# FRUITS
## *of the*
# SPIRIT

The 2002 Christian Companion

*Fruits of the Spirit*
Published by Foundery Press
© Trustees Methodist Church Purposes, 2001

ISBN  1 85852 207 2

Compiled by Susan Hibbins

Printed in Great Britain by Stanley Hunt Limited

# CONTENTS

# FOREWORD

'The wind blows where it will', says John's Gospel, using the word which also means Spirit. There is a wonderful variety, even randomness, about the prayers and poems, the sayings and stories in this book, coming as they do from different centuries, different continents, and reflecting all manner of experience. This is a book to browse with, a wide selection of gifts from brothers and sisters in Christ, who offer themselves as companions on our journey. They offer the fruits of their living and praying, and they speak to a very wide range of needs.

But it would be a great mistake *just* to browse, or to sample only what immediately appeals, or indeed to miss the underlying unity of this book. There is much here to sit down with and to ponder, seeking to be open to the Spirit who searches even the depths of God, and thus always has new truths to reveal. And there is a link far deeper than the book's uniting 'theme' of the fruits of the Spirit, though that is there for the tracing. There is the communion of saints who wrote and the saints who will read this *Companion*, and, please God, the communion of both with the God who by his Spirit gives all the gifts and brings all the harvest.

It is my privilege and pleasure to commend this *Companion*. May it bear much fruit.

Christina Le Moignan
President of the Methodist Conference, 2001-2002

# Transformation

# Grape Expectations

## Nigel Bovey

OOOF! For the umpteenth time that afternoon my fork struck the unforgiving London clay that is a less-than-compelling feature of our suburban Surrey back garden. My wife Margaret and I had moved in three years earlier, our sixth house in sixteen years as Salvation Army officers. One piece of advice which had stuck with me from our time in training college was about matters horticultural: 'Don't have the worst looking garden in the street.'

Over the years I'd changed from duty-bound weeder to enthusiastic potterer, spurred on by Geoffrey Hamilton's *Gardener's World* and Nature's stubborn refusal to let all my hand-sown seeds die.

Here I was, then, at the untouched part of our estate, excavating for dear life – turning the clay, digging in sharp sand and the free horse manure I'd negotiated from a local stables which, according to my wife, would stink the car out for weeks. This bottom right-hand corner of the garden was a sun-trap. Here I would plant my *pièce de résistance* – a vineyard. Well, OK, just a couple of vines. I'd long since fancied growing (and eating) my own grapes, but the climates of previous gardens in the likes of Londonderry, Liverpool and Worcester were not exactly sun-kissed Bordeaux.

This was take two. My first attempt the previous year had proved, quite literally, fruitless. I'd set two six-inch twigs fresh from the Jiffy bag in the wrong place (too shady) and the wrong soil (too scrubby). After a few more turns of the

fork, I committed the earth to the elements and downed tools for the day.

A month later I was back. The wind, rain and sun had broken up the soil sufficiently for me to dig two usable holes, now lined with compost and a sprinkling of fishblood and bone. (No idea what it does but I always think it looks impressive.) Time to take the plunge. Fork to foot, I eased the barely alive vines from their summer placements and pressed them into the newly prepared soil. Mallet in hand, I knocked in some old apple tree branches as stakes and strung some wire between them to support the tendrils that would burst forth in a few weeks' time. Or so the book said. Looking at the couple of watered-in twigs, I wasn't going to hold my breath.

As early spring showers gave way to early summer sunshine I had to erect more posts and wire. The vines had gone mad – forty feet long, seven feet high, they were a mass of vibrant foliage. The grotty interlapped fence behind them was hidden beneath curly fronds and huge green hands. I'd done it! I was growing vines.

In the November drizzle I stood, secateurs in hand. Before me, the last of the now-crimson vine leaves drooped defiantly as the wind gathered from the west. Rain trickled down the back of my Barbour. It was not a day for hanging about. The words of the gardening book, still open on the kitchen table, were fresh in my mind. 'Cut the vine back to three or four buds.'

But what if I got it wrong? What if I cut in the wrong place? I could kill the vine. I'd ruin a lovely summer display. I'd have to put something else in its place and it would take years to cover the fence again. I agonised. Who said gardening was relaxing?

I went back inside the house. Fortified by a cup of coffee, two digestives and another read of my gardening book, I returned to the bottom of the garden. Was I happy with just a show of leaves or did I want fruit? If coverage was all I was after I could opt to do nothing. But the book was clear: if I wanted the chance of fruit I'd have to do some serious cutting back.

Make-your-mind-up time, Nigel. I went for fruit.

Barely able to watch, I wrapped the secateurs around the main stem, three buds up. It was now or never. Taking faith in both hands, I tentatively squeezed the blades together. Snip! It was done. The point of no return.

Twenty minutes later I was committing the cuttings to the compost heap. Looking at the pathetic twigs sprouting from their horse manure beds, I was swamped with worry. Had I done the right thing? Did I cut too much off? Too late now. Only time would tell.

Winter frosts and spring rain delivered my answer. The vines burst into life, curling their way around the strategically placed wires, draping themselves across my neighbour's fence. Then, one day in summer, while hoeing the nearby veg plot, I caught sight of what looked like a cluster of tiny green marbles. 'Maggie!' I shouted. My wife, thinking something was wrong, flung open the kitchen door and with a 'What on earth's the matter?' came dashing down the garden.

'Grapes!'

By the end of that sunny summer we were picking plump ripe fruit for all we were worth. Most of it never made it into the fruit bowl. The black juicy grapes tasted a treat. And all grown naturally, not a greenhouse or cloche in sight!

That's the thing about nature, we can't control it, we can't fight it, we can only co-operate with it. And the thing about fruit is, when conditions are right – and you follow the book – it grows naturally. In fact, we can't stop it growing. That's what fruit does.

Spirit of God, descend upon my heart;
Wean it from earth; through all its pulses move;
Stoop to my weakness, mighty as thou art,
And make me love thee as I ought to love.

I ask no dream, no prophet ecstasies,
No sudden rending of the veil of clay,
No angel visitant, no opening skies,
But take the dimness of my soul away.

Teach me to feel that thou art always nigh;
Teach me the struggles of the soul to bear;
To check the rising doubt, the rebel sigh;
Teach me the patience of unanswered prayer.

Teach me to love thee as thine angels love,
One holy passion filling all my frame;
The kindling of the heaven descended Dove,
My heart an altar, and thy love the flame.

George Croly

The moment of failure and humiliation can be the moment of greatest advance, when it is discovered that the Spirit is guiding towards an attitude of trust in the words and way of Jesus as a genuine revelation of the nature of God. Though outward circumstances may collapse, and relationships fail, the way of Jesus can sustain the weight of a person's life as s/he commits it in trust. The journey of the Spirit is to make in every new situation that step of faith.

John White

Look on us, O Lord, and let all the darkness of our souls disappear before the beams of your brightness. Fill us with your holy love, and open to us the treasures of your wisdom. You know all our desire, so bring to perfection what you have started and what your Spirit has awakened us to ask in prayer. We seek your face; turn your face to us and show us your glory. Then our longing will be satisfied, and our peace will be perfect.

St. Augustine

God will never plant the seed of his life upon the soil of a hard, unbroken spirit. He will only plant that seed where the conviction of his Spirit has brought brokenness, where the soil has been watered with the tears of repentance as well as the tears of joy.

Alan Redpath

*Every time we say, 'I believe in the Holy Spirit', we mean that we believe that there is a living God able to enter human personality and change it.*

*J. B. Phillips*

The human soul is a silent harp in God's choir whose strings need only to be swept by the divine breath to chime with the harmonies of creation.

Henry David Thoreau

For the power thou hast given me to lay
    hold of things unseen;
For the strong sense I have that this is
    not my home:
For my restless heart that nothing finite
    can satisfy:
I give thee thanks, O God.
For the invasion of my soul by thy Holy
    Spirit:
For all the human love and goodness
    that speak to me of thee:
For the fullness of thy glory outpoured
    in Jesus Christ:
I give thee thanks, O God.

John Baillie

Let us pray God that he would root out of our hearts
everything of our own planting and set out there, with his
own hand, the tree of life bearing all manner of fruits.

Francois Fenelon

*Silence is not an end in itself, but a means to a higher experience.
It is the opportunity, not only for prayerful meditation for the
unfolding of truth and the apprehension of duty, but for the
realisation of the divine forgiveness, the renewal of our wills and
the upbuilding of our inward being in communion with the
divine love.*

*Friends' Book of Discipline*

God of all peace and consolation, grant us the gift of your
Spirit to enlighten, refresh, enable and sanctify our souls:
to be over and around us as the light and dew of heaven,
and to fit us  for whatever work you are calling us to do;
through Jesus Christ our Lord.

Source unknown

*Deep in every heart there is an innermost room.  To some it is a
place unvisited and unknown; to others it is a place dim with
shadows and haunted by tears.  But if we will but have it so, this
innermost room may be the place of God's presence.  There the
peace of God may always be waiting for us.*

*Francis B. James*

# The Journey into Wholeness

# Donald Eadie

> He who attempts to act and to do anything
> for others or for the world without
> deepening his own self-understanding,
> freedom, integrity and capacity to love will
> not have anything to give others.[1]

In my writing about the fruits of the Spirit I want to draw
on the tradition that discerns the Spirit breathing
throughout the whole of our humanity and forming slowly
and secretly. 'Above all, trust the slow work of God.'[2]
Fruits take time to form and similarly, to change the
metaphor, journeys take time to complete, and there are
journeys within journeys.

I live in Birmingham and am part of a group that includes
people who have travelled the world. Some are now
alongside refugees and asylum seekers, engaged with
environmental issues, with the peace movement and with
a variety of community projects. What happens when we
meet? We listen to each other's stories of reconciliation,
encourage each other and reflect on the nature of
reconciliation itself. We learn the enrichment which
comes from acknowledging that which is 'other' within
our differences. We explore the complex relationship
between our inner and outer worlds. We grow in
awareness of our human tendency to project elsewhere the
dark within each of us, the bits that we find it hard to
accept, the bits we don't like. Slowly, and at times
painfully, we are recognising the need to embrace this
perplexing interacting mixture of good and evil, light and
shadow, creation and destruction as belonging to the

wonder and terror of who we are. We are discovering that not only can the wounds from the past fester, disfigure and imprison but they can also be gathered into our journey and become part of our greater wholeness. To embrace this reality is to begin the journey towards a wholeness that contains a hidden healing.

What are we learning? We are searching for a common human language through which we are able to express that which is sacred and life-giving, that which belongs to the deep things of life and death. We are recognising the dangers of separating opposites that essentially belong together. And we are discovering the potential in befriending the dark. There is a darkness within seedtime leading to harvest. The grave and the womb are also dark. Some are awake and in pain in the early hours of the morning, others nurse the newborn and some keep their nightly watch.

> While darkness covers the earth
> And all the world sleeps
> We open our hearts to the mysteries of God.[3]

Mary Grey writes of the potential in befriending the dark:

> . . . to claim back the night is to claim darkness as a time for growth and transformation. It is to free darkness of its overtones of evil and sin and see it as potential richness, fertility, hidden growth and contemplation, as nature broods and contemplates in winter, seemingly inactive, yet preparing for the birthing of spring. It is in darkness that new vision is born . . .[4]

So this is where we are, this is where we explore, this is where we are pilgrims and this is where we meet God. The divine presence is discovered through encounter, not proposition. We trust in the One who is mysteriously present in all things, in our reality, in our circumstance and not separate, contained within some religious department.

12

'God is as the breath inside the breath, the source of all that is life-giving.'[5]

Some of us have lived in the belief that God is outside, up there, one who rescues us from ourselves and the world. These images are no longer adequate and we search for new ones. God, we discover, is not a push-button God, sliding down a slippery pole from heaven but rather present and nudging within the membranes of life. A man in old age uttered a startling prayer that finds its echoes in us: 'God: rid us of this God!' There has been a need for God to be liberated from our religious notions of God and rediscovered within life as mystery, as surprise, as a source of wisdom, truth, being . . . God is greater than God seems. Immanence is held within and is not separate from transcendence.

The search for God in all things is not for intellectual understanding but rather for encouragement to enter and explore what it could mean to say, 'God is in all things' even when it doesn't feel like it or look like it. All things? In the sordid? In the hideous evil in Auschwitz, in Rwanda? Is it make-believe? Is it self-deception? The Bible speaks not only of God as the unknowable God who is our rock and our refuge but also as the God of Jesus who transforms evil into good:

> We are not offered salvation from an evil situation, but salvation in and through an evil situation, first confronting it, then bearing it, and transforming it. It is as if evil is the raw material out of which new life is forged . . . Jesus is less interested in the causes of evil than in its transformation.[6]

It is possible to trust when totally baffled. Whilst living with inoperable cancer Bishop John Robinson preached his last sermon in October 1983 in Trinity College Chapel, Cambridge. He said:

> Two years ago I found myself having to speak at the funeral of a sixteen year old girl who died in our Yorkshire dale. I said stumblingly that God was to be found in the cancer as much as in the sunset. That I firmly believed, but it was an intellectual statement. Now I have had to ask if I can say it for myself, which is a much greater test.[7]

All I can pray is 'God be God in this place . . . God show me your face' and then wait. I live with words from Simone Weil: 'The only power that God has in this world is the love he inspires in us. That is the only power on offer.'[8]

The journey towards wholeness with its labyrinthine paths, both inner and outer, is, for me, the fruit of the Spirit for which I give thanks. It incorporates all those other fruits in the well-known biblical text.[9]

---

1    From the writing of Thomas Merton.
2    From a poem discovered in the personal correspondence of Teilhard de Chardin. The translator is unknown.
3    From some words for night prayer by Sandy Ryrie.
4    Mary Grey, *Redeeming the Dream*, published by Gujarat Sahitya Prakash.
5    Mary Grey, *Beyond the Dark Night*, Cassell.
6    Michael Wilson, 'God of love and evil', an unpublished essay.
7    'Learning from Cancer' p.189 in John Robinson, *Last Essays and Sermons*, SCM Press.
8    'Intercession in the context of the Holocaust', Rabbi Lionel Blue, *The Tablet*.
9    Galatians 5: 22-26.

*He rode at furious speed to Broken Edge,*
*And he was very angry, very small;*
*But God was kind, knowing he needed not*
*A scolding, nor a swift unpleasant fall,*
*Nor any high reproach of soul at all.*
*'It matters not,' said Reason and Good Sense;*
*'Absurd to let a trifle grow immense.'*
*'It matters very much,' said Busy Brain;*
*'You cannot be content and calm again,*
*For you are angry in a righteous cause.'*
*'Poor, queer old Waxy!' laughed the hips and haws.*
*'God has a sense of humour,' said a ball*
*Of orange-gold inside a spindle-berry –*
*And "Christe our Lord is full and exceeding merrie." '*

*He lingered in the lane at Broken Edge,*
*Bryony berries burned from every hedge;*
*Snails in the deep wet grass of fairy rings*
*Told him of unimaginable things.*
*Love was in all the colours of the sky,*
*Love in the folded shadows of the high*
*Blue hills, as quiet as any Easter Eve.*
*(O fool, O blind and earthbound thus to grieve!)*

*He turned his horse. Through level sunset-gleams*
*He saw a little road that curled*
*And climbed elusive to a sky of dreams.*
*His anger over Broken Edge was hurled*
*To scatter into nothing on a gust*
*Of wind which brought the twilight to the trees.*
*The drifted leaves, the white October dust*
*Hiding the beechnuts for the squirrel's store,*
*Heard the low whisper spoken on his knees –*
*'God, you have made a very perfect world,*
*Don't let me spoil it ever any more.'*

*V. L. Edminson*

In the hour of willing surrender to the reality of Holiness, a flood of quite unutterable joy swept over me; a boundless sense of power came streaming into my soul, with a sensation of almost physical cleansing and refreshing.

Anonymous

Father, thou must lead:
Do thou, then, breathe those thoughts into my mind
By which such virtue may in me be bred,
That in thy holy footsteps I may tread;
The fetters of my tongue do thou unbind,
That I may have the power to sing of thee
And sound thy praises everlastingly.

Michelangelo

Wonderful as the sun is, is not he who made it more wonderful? Glorious as is the returning of spring to light, what about that Light that 'never was on sea or land', that can burst with sudden radiance upon the inward eye? Suppose the orbit of your being were to swing into a really harmonious relationship with the Spirit of God, so that your purposes blended and your ways became more identified?

Albert D. Belden

*People may tire themselves in a labyrinth of search, and talk of God; but if we would know him indeed, it must be from the impressions we receive of him; and the softer our hearts are, the deeper and livelier those will be upon us.*

*William Penn*

The Holy Spirit is the invisible third party who stands between me and the other, making us mutually aware. Supremely and primarily he opens my eyes to Christ. But he also opens my eyes to the brother [and sister] in Christ . . . or the point of need, or the heartbreaking beauty of the world. He is the giver of that vision without which the people perish. We so commonly speak about him as the source of *power*. But in fact he enables us not by making us supernaturally strong but by opening our eyes.

John Taylor

We cannot expect to be able to give a precise description of the way God transforms our stubborn hearts and purifies our selfish desires. We cannot know how God does his own work and we need not be able to understand his ways in order to experience his transforming power. He transforms us by inhabiting our lives and the fruits of his labours begin to appear in the lives of those who 'become the place wherein the Holy Spirit makes his dwelling'.

Ronald Spivey

*Let us labour for an inward stillness*
*An inward stillness and an inward healing;*
*That perfect silence where the lips and heart*
*Are still, and we no longer entertain*
*Our own imperfect thoughts and vain opinions,*
*But God alone speaks in us, and we wait*
*In singleness of heart that we may know*
*His will . . .*

*H. W. Longfellow*

. . . What we must be clear about is that God himself is our teacher, and it is his Spirit that awakens ours . . . God will reach us but he will give us only what we are able to take at the time, little by little. It may be just a sentence, one word even, that touches us . . . and that will act as a springboard for reflection, perhaps offering enlightenment in some new way.

Delia Smith

The outpouring of his Holy Spirit is really the outpouring of his love, surrounding and penetrating your little soul with a peaceful, joyful delight in his creature: tolerant, peaceful, a love full of long-suffering and gentleness, working quietly, able to wait for results, faithful, devoted, without variableness or shadow of turning. Such is the charity of God . . .

Love breaks down the barrier that shuts most of us out of heaven. That thought is too much for us really . . . yet it is the central truth of the spiritual life. And that loving, self-yielding to the Eternal Love – that willingness that God shall possess, indwell, fertilise, bring forth fruit of *his* Spirit in us instead of fruits of our Spirit – is the secret of all Christian power and all Christian peace.

Evelyn Underhill

# The Transforming Spirit

# Peter Stephens

In writing to the Galatians Paul contrasts the Spirit with the flesh and the law. We shall understand what he says on the fruit of the Spirit better, if we see how he contrasts the Spirit with the flesh (5:16-17, 19-24) and the law (5:18).

## The Spirit and the Flesh

When we speak of the flesh and the Spirit we often think of the flesh as outward and the Spirit as inward. That makes us think of the works of the flesh as outward and physical. But for Paul the flesh is not something outward and physical but refers to the whole person as self-centred. Therefore works of the flesh can be inward like jealousy, and not only outward like drunkenness (5:19-20).

The flesh, therefore, stands not for outward things, but for human beings as sinful or self-centred. Left to ourselves we find it natural to put ourselves in the centre of our life. That self-centredness leads us automatically to seek our own good rather than the good of others. For Paul, when people become Christians as the Galatians had done, they become part of a new community in which the Holy Spirit, not the flesh, is at work. That for Paul is the great new fact in the life of Christians. There is a new dynamic in their life. When the Spirit is at work in people he begins to produce a new life which is centred not in us but in Christ, a life which reflects, however imperfectly, the life of Jesus. Paul opposes these two different ways of life in his contrast between the works of the flesh and the fruit of the Spirit.

Just as we can misunderstand what is spiritual by identifying it with what is inward, we can also misunderstand it by identifying it with what is religious. Thus we think of going to church, or singing hymns, or reading the Bible as spiritual. By contrast we think of going to the cinema rather than to church, singing pop songs rather than hymns, or reading novels rather than the Bible as unspiritual.

Besides thinking that religious things are spiritual, we may even think that some religious things are more spiritual than others. Thus we speak of praise and prayer as spiritual, but we consider making the tea, visiting the sick, or clearing away the trestle tables as not spiritual, or not as spiritual as prayer and praise.

Now I would not want in any way to undervalue praying, praising, and reading the Bible. They are vital in the Christian life. We may describe them as religious or devotional, but we must beware of describing them as spiritual, as though they have to do with the Spirit, whereas our work, our leisure, or our practical service are not to do with the Spirit. Indeed, singing hymns to see if you can lift the roof may be much more unspiritual than singing rowdy pop songs.

Paul helps us to see that what is unspiritual (or fleshly) is not a particular activity, but a self-centred attitude leading to a self-centred act. For example, the activity of sex is not in itself fleshly or unspiritual, but the self-centred attitude which leads to sexual immorality is. The activity of drinking is not in itself fleshly or unspiritual, but the self-centred attitude which leads to drunkenness is. The activity of disagreeing is not in itself fleshly or unspiritual, but the self-centred attitude which leads to party spirit is.

Our churches are not full of some of the works of the flesh, which Paul describes in 5:19-20, such as sorcery, drunkenness, and carousing. But what about some of the others – jealousy, anger, dissension, and party spirit? Consider the reaction when someone occupies your normal seat or parking place, when a newcomer is elected to the church council and not your husband, or when a commission decides to unite your church with another one on their site and not on yours! These actions spring not from the Holy Spirit but from our self-centredness. They are works of the flesh, not the fruit of the Spirit.

## The Spirit and the Law

Paul said many things about the law in Galatians, but especially he attacked the way many Jews insisted on the necessity of obeying the law to win God's favour. He saw that as living like a slave, striving to win the favour of his master. He contrasted this with the life of a son, who is sure of his father's love and does not have to win it by what he does.

The Jews believed that if the Gentiles were to become part of God's people they must accept and keep the law, which God had given to the Jews centuries before. Paul challenged this. He insisted that Gentile Christians had become part of God's people through God's grace in Christ, not through keeping God's law. (A proof of this is the fact that they had received the Spirit promised to God's people.) They did not need to keep the law to win God's acceptance. God had accepted them. They were not slaves, but sons – with the freedom of sons.

Freedom was a risky message for people who had so recently been deeply pagan – superstitious in their religion, dissolute in their morals. Surely freedom from the law for such people would lead to licence. No, said Paul. That would be another form of slavery, being slaves to their self-centred desires. When they became Christians they were baptised into Christ. That meant that they belonged to Christ. Moreover they were given the Holy Spirit and what the Holy Spirit did was to enable people to live like Christ. The fruit of the Spirit is love. It is significant that you can sum up the whole law in the word love (5:14) and love is the fruit of the Spirit. Therefore Christians energised by the Spirit are enabled to fulfil the law. They fulfil it not as a way of winning God's favour and avoiding his judgement, but because they are united to the God who is love. The law is about our striving to do God's will in order to gain his acceptance. Paul's message is not about a God whose love needs to be won, but of the God who has accepted us in Christ and whose Spirit has become the new dynamic in our lives.

## The Fruit of the Spirit is Love . . .

We use the word love in many ways. We talk of loving our children, or loving our girlfriends, or loving fish and chips. We mean that we like or we are fond of someone or something. But that is not the meaning of love in the New Testament. It uses love of Christ and says that we really see what love is in his life and death (1 John 3:16). His is not a love that seeks its own (1 Corinthians 13:5), but a love that gives itself to others. His love is, moreover, not love for a few – those close to him, those who love him, or those who deserve his love. It is love to the loveless shown, a love for those who are self-centred (Romans 5:8).

How do you and I begin to love like that? It is as we are captured by his love. It is as we are loved by him without deserving it that we begin to become free to love (1 John 4:19). Indeed, we find something similar with ordinary human love. For example, it is as we are loved by our parents when we are children that we become able to risk ourselves in love as we grow up. It is something like that with the amazing love of God, which we see in Jesus. That love which we see supremely on the cross can draw us to him and transform us. This is not something *we* do. It is what the Spirit does in us, drawing us to Christ and uniting us with him. That is why it can be spoken of as both the work of Christ and the fruit of the Spirit.

## If we live by the Spirit, let us also walk by the Spirit

Paul speaks at points as if everything happens automatically. When he writes of faith in Christ as active in love (5:6), we may think that once we believe in Christ or are united with him then we shall love – and that's that. But it does not happen as easily as that or at least not for most of us. We are those to whom Paul (and most preachers) say, 'Become what you are. You are a Christian; live like a Christian.' 'If the Spirit is the source of our life, let the Spirit also direct our course' or 'If we live by the Spirit, let us also walk by the Spirit' (5:25). How will this happen? By putting to death our self-centred desires and by focusing anew on Christ, trusting ourselves afresh to his Spirit.

One way of doing this is by recalling those whose lives show us something of ourselves and something of Christ. They help us to see how we are still centred in ourselves and they make us realise how much we have still to do to put our self-centred nature to death. But also by what they do or say they show us something of Christ. That can challenge and inspire us to surrender ourselves anew to him and let his Spirit renew and transform us.

Let me give you just one example, an example of love. It is a story from the beginning of the twentieth century when thousands of Armenians were killed by the Turks in appalling acts of genocide.

A Turkish officer raided and looted an Armenian home. He killed the aged parents and gave the daughters to the soldiers, keeping the eldest daughter for himself. Some time later she escaped and trained as a nurse. As time passed she found herself nursing in a ward of Turkish officers. One night by the light of a lantern she saw the face of this officer. He was so gravely ill that without exceptional nursing he would die. The days passed and he recovered. One day the doctor stood by the bed with her and said to him, 'But for her devotion to you, you would be dead.' He looked at her and said, 'We have met before, haven't we?' 'Yes', she said, 'we have met before.' 'Why didn't you kill me?' he asked. She replied, 'I am a follower of him who said, "Love your enemies." '

As we focus on Christ, or think of those whose lives are most like his, we can be drawn anew to him and be enabled by his Spirit both to put to death the flesh (our self-centred nature) and to walk by the Spirit.

*Spirit of God*
*Reaching down to the very depths of our being*
*Dancing to life's ebb and flow.*

*Spirit of God*
*Latent in all creation, dancing in the wind*
*Casting your light.*

*Spirit of God*
*Present in the Trinity, burst forth within us*
*And dance in our lives.*

*Stella Bristow & Rosemary Wass*

I am he, the power and goodness of fatherhood; I am he
the wisdom and lovingness of motherhood; I am he, the
light and grace which is all blessed love . . . I am he, the
great supreme goodness of every kind of thing; I am he
who makes you to love.

Dame Julian of Norwich

Christianity is the most encouraging, the most joyous, the least repressive, the least forbidding of all the religions of humankind. There is no religion which throws off the burden of life so completely, which escapes so swiftly from our moods, which gives so large a scope for the high spirits of humankind. It is always music that you hear, and sometimes dancing as well.

L. P. Jacks

The wind bloweth where it listeth: thou canst not tell whence it cometh or whither it goeth. So it is with everyone that is born of the Spirit. Invisibly, silently, gently, the life of the Spirit and the Spirit of life enter into the soul.

J. A. Clapperton

When you come to Christ, the Holy Spirit takes up residence in your heart. Something new is added to your life supernaturally. You are transformed by the renewing of your mind. A new power, a new dimension, a new ability to love, a new joy, a new peace – the Holy Spirit comes in and lives the Christian life through you.

Billy Graham

*To accept the will of God never leads to the miserable feeling that it is useless to strive any more. God does not ask for the dull, weak, sleepy acquiescence of indolence. He asks for something vivid and strong. He asks us to co-operate with him, actively willing what he wills, our only aim his glory.*

*Amy Carmichael*

I have learned to place myself before God every day as a vessel to be filled with his Holy Spirit. He has filled me with the blessed assurance that he, as everlasting God, has guaranteed his own work in me.

Andrew Murray

*The energies of the Holy Spirit put the emphasis upon 'I can'. It is a moment-by-moment life . . . He abides with them. Their characters are planned, shaped, built by the Spirit.*

*W. E. Sangster*

Humans' work is accompanied by so much noise; if they desire a silver cup for sacraments there must go to its fashioning the sound of hammering, the scratch of a chisel, the roar of a furnace; but when the innumerable chalices of the privet are made ready for the hawk-moth's first taste of honey, there is no stir at all. The aisles and transepts of our temples rise with the clamour of voices and commotion of labour . . . but the aisles of pines down a mountainside, the transept of beeches in a valley, rise as softly as thought into majestic completeness. A crocus achieves her end; her curving cup stands up in the light and air, in spite of the weight of inanimate matter pressing on her from all sides during her upward progress; with thin petals folded close in the delicate pointed face, she comes through unscathed and silent.

Mary Webb

Under the influence of the blessed Spirit, faith produces holiness, and holiness strengthens faith.

Juan Valera

*The bright wind is blowing, the bright wind of heaven,*
*And where it is going to, no-one can say;*
*But where it is passing our hearts are awaking*
*To grope from the darkness and reach for the day.*

*The bright wind is blowing, the bright wind of heaven,*
*And many old thoughts will be winnowed away;*
*The husk that is blown on the chaff of our hating,*
*The seed that is left is the hope for our day.*

*The bright wind is blowing, the bright wind of heaven,*
*The love that it kindles will never betray;*
*That fire that it fans is the warmth of our caring,*
*So lean on the wind – it will show us the way.*

*Cecily Taylor*

Spiritual processes, as a rule, cannot be seen. There is a great mystery about the divinest things in life. God's mightiest forces are secret forces. God's greatest works are operations in which the hand of the Worker is hid.

R. A. Finlayson

# Fruits from Within

# Maureen Edwards

*The following imaginary letter is based on Romans 16:1-16 and the wishful, though unlikely, link with Mark 15:21.*

The first century church in Rome, 'set apart for the Gospel of God', to God's beloved, 'called to be saints' in the twenty-first century: 'Grace to you and peace from God our Father and the Lord Jesus Christ.'

First, we give thanks for your faithfulness to the Gospel of our Lord Jesus Christ in an age of doubt and changing moral standards. We don't know how you cope! No wonder you are concerned about how to follow in the way of Christ, and how to develop a deeper spirituality so that the 'fruits of the Spirit' may be seen in you. 'Love, joy, peace, patience, kindness, generosity, faithfulness, gentleness and self-control.' What a list! We only wish we could say that they are seen in us, and yet they do appear in the most surprising places.

As you can imagine we have some exceptional people here. Rome is that sort of city: for us, it is the centre of the world, full of history, fine architecture, culture, sport ... Like the great cities of your day it draws talent of all kinds; it is cosmopolitan, excitingly varied, challenging ... And so is our church life. Some of the Christians, who've come from other places and settled here, may not be wealthy, but the quality of their lives has enriched us beyond measure. And, of course, many of them even met the living Jesus: they listened to his teaching, talked with him, helped him; they certainly saw the fruits of the Spirit in him and were changed by all they received from him.

31

One of them is Rufus. His father was Simon of Cyrene –
the African who carried the cross for Jesus to Golgotha.
His mother, who overflows with joy and the spirit of
hospitality, has 'mothered' many Christian leaders and
fellow-workers, including the apostle Paul. Nothing is too
much for her. She can always make room in her home for
one more, and she has that rare gift of making you feel like
an 'honoured guest'. So has Rufus. Unlike his father,
Rufus has taken up the cross of his own free will. It isn't
easy to be a Christian here. Christians are suspect in
Roman society. At the moment there is no outright
persecution, but we guard our freedom with care and
share the anguish of those who have suffered in other
places and, of course, the story of Rufus' father Simon is
often told.

Simon had gone up to Jerusalem for the Passover and
heard Jesus in the Temple. There was something so
compelling about Jesus, he said. For the first time in his
life, Simon was deeply challenged. Jesus' faith and
integrity, his strength of love and truth itself were so
obvious in all he said. Simon followed, listening, getting
more and more angry at the bigotry of those who were
trying to eliminate Jesus . . . And so he was carried along
with the crowd on that fateful Friday morning. You know
the rest of the story, how when Jesus stumbled under the
weight of the cross, Simon was grabbed by a Roman
soldier and forced to carry Jesus' cross. For a second, he
almost refused, protesting against the power of the Roman
oppressor.

Then, in a matter of seconds, it was as though he was
catapulted into the suffering of the world. Instead of
striking back at his exploiter, he found himself helping
Jesus to carry upon his shoulders the suffering of those
who are unjustly sentenced to death, raped, tortured, even
little children massacred by death squads, ordinary people
whose homes are destroyed in war, unwanted asylum
seekers . . . It seemed as though he had been forced to

forget himself and the fairly easy, unchallenged life he had led before to share the lives of others, to identify with them, to share their struggle. For that is God's way. It was a strange, unnerving experience. Simon saw all the vulnerability of God in Jesus – God who is revealed in ways that the world counts foolish; God whose love and gentleness are seen in the silence and impotence of the cross; God whose death turns upside-down all the remedies the world offers to deal with human sin and violence; God who, through this death, cleanses us in a way that no one else can . . . Simon was profoundly changed and so are others who get to know him. This is indeed the work of the Spirit.

That reminds us of Andronicus and Junias, Paul's relatives. They were converted even before Paul and they have worked from the beginning with the apostles. Like Paul, they have risked their lives for the sake of the Gospel, and even suffered imprisonment. On one occasion they were in prison with Paul himself. This is the price of faithfulness to Christ. The greatest gift, says Paul, is love, and love will go to great lengths to be faithful. With Christ, like Simon of Cyrene, we enter into the suffering of others.

Aquila and his wife Prisca, two other notable Christians in Rome, were also caught up in this kind of tension. In the year 49 AD, when the Emperor Claudius issued an edict expelling all Christians from Rome, they had to leave their home and set out not knowing where God would take them next. Nothing daunted them. Eventually they settled in Corinth where they met Paul and made a new life for themselves. Paul lodged with them and that was the beginning of a long partnership. They had so much in common: the same love for people, the same joy in proclaiming the good news, the same resilience in face of persecution, the same vision of a universal church . . . They are such an interesting couple, always ready to take risks for the sake of the Gospel. We owe so much to their enthusiasm and energy. We hope they will stay here, but it's more likely they'll want to respond to opportunities to witness in other places.

Like Paul, Aquila is a tent-maker by trade. Aquila and Prisca are friendly, hospitable and generous. They have a deep faith and are well-informed. Paul knows he can rely on them, especially Prisca, to share their faith with others. It was Prisca and Aquila who taught Apollos, that great preacher who made such an impression on the church in Corinth. They have never actually travelled with Paul on his journeys, but their paths often cross, and Paul knows that he can depend on them to help and to offer shelter to others.

Paul includes 'hospitality' in his list of spiritual gifts. We cannot underestimate the importance of this ministry. It has a dynamic that not only builds fellowship and helps the traveller and the lonely, but those of us who have opened our homes have made so many friends. This is particularly so in a city like Rome where people from all over the world come and go. We listen to one another's stories, share our problems, our hopes and dreams. And so we catch fresh insights, our faith is deepened as we learn from others, and we know that Christ is present in all of this.

In case you think it's all deadly serious, we would assure you that we have lots of fun. Sometimes we roll around laughing at some of the funny things that happen to us all! There is a fine line between laughter and pain. They are mysteriously interwoven in our lives. That is how God made us. Jesus too had lots of fun. He loved parties. And so it was, we think, that at the Last Supper, he took the food and wine of hospitality, fun and fellowship and made them symbols of his brokenness, affirming that all the love and laughter that had gone before were indestructible. This is the nature of that fruit of the Spirit called 'Joy'. It's not an effervescent, bubbling euphoria; it doesn't ignore the grief and pain we suffer, but enables us to face the difficulties, sometimes to rise above them, and to know that God is present in all the experiences we go through. In such a way we are to 'rejoice with those who rejoice and weep with those who weep'.

We pray for you – that the Spirit will lead you out to cross all kinds of barriers to discover Christ where he is mostly to be found – among people at the bottom: the poor, the isolated, the despised . . . There are many we could tell you about: faithful, loving and caring people, and we thank God for them all. 'By their fruits you shall know them,' said Jesus, and we do. Poor, according to the world's estimation, they are indeed rich. Their generosity, their unaffected love and kindness, their joy – all these fruits come from within. They are people of prayer, always cherishing that inner space which the Spirit fills with all that is pure, good, peaceful, loving . . . Of such is the kingdom. We all greet you, and we rejoice with you in the surprising ways the Spirit challenges you in the twenty-first century. We pray that you will infect the world with the gifts and fruits that the Spirit nurtures within you. May God's love sustain you, the grace of Christ enfold you and the movement of the Spirit involve you in the life of the kingdom. Amen.

*But I can neither write nor tell of what sort of exaltation the triumphing in the Spirit is. It can be compared with naught, but that when in the midst of death life is born, and it is like the resurrection of the dead.*

*Jacob Boehme*

Grant to your servants, O God,
To be set on fire with your love
To be strengthened by your power
To be illuminated by your Spirit
To be filled with your grace
And to go forward by your help
Through Christ our Lord.

Gallican Sacramentary

May God, the Fountain of all blessing, fill us with the understanding of sacred knowledge. May he keep us sound in faith, steadfast in hope, and persevering in patient charity.

A Chain of Prayer across the Ages

How do you describe the indescribable? The people who started the church in motion on a day of Pentecost in Jerusalem used symbols, picture language to convey what they could not describe . . . If the symbols are helpful they will convey the sense of wonder, of awakening, of a Spirit in ourselves that impels us towards the Spirit that moves the universe. And for us, too, the activity of the Spirit may be seen in an increase of awareness and sensitivity, of a deeper love and a greater joy, of creative communities which exist to serve others.

Peter D. Bishop

This sense of connection between inner growth and outer change permeates the Christian understanding of reality. St. Paul was an activist of the first order. Every time he entered a new place he created major disruptions, but his activism was the fruit of the relationship he enjoyed with the living Christ . . . The ministries of Mother Teresa in the slums of Calcutta or of Martin Luther King in the streets of Montgomery, or of the countless people whose faith has touched your life and mine and indeed has affected the life of the world are expressions of lived prayer.

James Fenhagen

*Take from us, O God,*
*All pride and vanity,*
*All boasting and forwardness*
*And give us true courage that shows itself by gentleness;*
*The true wisdom that shows itself by simplicity;*
*And the true power that shows itself by modesty;*
*Through Jesus Christ our Lord.*

*Charles Kingsley*

God in Christ acts through the Holy Spirit to transform us from the inside out. This is not just a change in a few specific behaviours or personal habits. It is a fundamental reorientation of who we are.

Thomas R. Hawkins

Forgive us, Lord, that we have left the ground untilled, expecting an easy harvest. Help us to prepare our minds and hearts that the seed of thy love may grow in every part of our life, so that we bear fruit in thy service.

Anonymous

God, bring beauty and colour to my life.
Give me Christian qualities which are fresh and
      crisp,
nourishing and refreshing, and full of goodness.
Sow seeds in my life to bring your life to others –
new growth and new fruit.
Bring every little sign of life into flower, and let
      them blossom
to your glory.
Feed me day by day with your goodness.
Let me be rooted in your love.
Let me breathe your Spirit, and bask in the
      sunshine of your grace,
so that I may grow healthy in every way,
and so that the fruit of your Spirit may ripen in
      me.

David J. Winwood

*It is the great work of nature to transmute sunlight into life. So is the great end of Christian living to transmute the light of truth into the fruits of holy living.*

*Adoniram J. Gordon*

I went to the parish church for Evensong. The whole scene is indelibly impressed upon my memory. I sat in the second pew from the pulpit. I paid little attention to the service and less to the sermon which was preached by the curate. But I had a strong sense that something was about to happen. I was not in the least excited; there was no sort of nervous attention; I had only prayed in a rather weary way during the service in some such manner as this – 'I can't go on with this strange struggle. End it, O God, one way or another.' Then suddenly, while the unheeded went on, I was gripped by a clear conviction. It had all the strength of a masterful inward voice. 'You are wanted. You are called. You must obey.' I knew at once the thing was settled. The burden of long struggle dropped. My mind was free. I don't want to write emotionally, but it is only recording fact to say that a wave of peace and indeed joy as I had never known before filled my whole being.

Cosmo Gordon Lang

When we turn to God, when his pardon cancels our sin, and when his Spirit begins the new life within us, ours is a foretaste of heaven. And this life becomes what it ought to be, an opportunity to grow, to let God have his way with us.

Leslie Davison

# From Sorrow to Joy

# Julian M. Pursehouse

On 6th December 1997, I walked into the Gervis Pearson Ward of the City Hospital, Nottingham. I was met by an ashen-faced doctor who sat me down and promptly told me that my wife had passed away. One is never quite prepared for the moment when the news of death is broken; even though Regina had been suffering from an incurable disease for the last four years, the news hit me like a shocking bolt. My sense of shock was compounded by the awful reality of Regina's tender years – she was just thirty when she died. Young people are not meant to waste away and die!

For a few moments I sat by her bedside looking at the person who had been my wife, my best friend, my lover, my soul mate and the best thought at the beginning of each day. Tears streamed down my face and I felt utterly alone and bereft in a world where people would continue to laugh, young couples would still hold hands, congregations would continue to sing praises to God and people would expect me – a presbyter in the Methodist Church – to pull myself together and get on with life. I would discover later how difficult it is to express grief in such a public profession.

Over the next two years I spent my time gradually coming to terms with grief and separation. I discovered that there is no prescription for loss; there are no neat solutions or quick remedies that give one a fast track to healing and wholeness. The grieving soul must confront moments of profound darkness, endure feelings of utter desolation and experience intense emotional pain before rediscovering hope and joy. One of my overriding memories of this period of time was the intense energy that I needed to exert in order to fulfil the most common aspects of everyday existence. I had to force myself to get up, get dressed, eat, shop, clean, wash and all the other humdrum aspects of normal everyday life.

During this time of grieving I read a marvellous book entitled *As it is in Heaven* by Niall Williams. It is a life-affirming story of the struggle towards love and healing in the face of human tragedy. The story centres on Stephen Griffin (a schoolteacher) and his father Philip (a tailor) who are bound together by a common and profound sense of grief. Philip's wife and daughter have died tragically in a car crash three years previously, and he longs to be reunited with his family in heaven. Stephen yearns for love and pursues an Italian violinist named Gabriela Castoldi, and this gives both men a purpose in life: Stephen to capture the love of Gabriela, and Philip to aid him in this task by tailoring the best suit for him to wear as he woos Gabriela. In the early chapters of the book there is a touching scene where Philip goes to see his GP, Tim Magrath, and attempts to describe the predicament of grief.

> 'I can't feel any joy,' he said.
> Tim Magrath said nothing. He felt the eyes of the patient staring at him for an answer, but was so surprised that he had to get up and look at the street outside. He watched the passing cars for a moment.
> 'My wife died. My daughter died with her.'
> The doctor felt a shiver of guilt run down his spine; he had heard of the crash, of course, but missed the funeral and then let the facts of it slip away beyond acknowledgement.
> 'It was three years ago,' Philip said, 'and it's just, I can't feel any joy. In anything. Maybe I'm not supposed to. But I just thought I'd

mention it to somebody.  I wonder will I? . . . I just can't seem to.'
He was not distressed; he spoke about it as if telling a mildly unusual facet of his diet.'[1]

As I read this moving story I felt that I was listening to the voice of my own experience.  Like Philip, I had not felt joy for a long time, but equally I did not feel that this was how things were supposed to be.  The story acted as a catalyst for my own journey towards healing and love.  I was determined to live again and to feel passionate about being human.

It began in a very simple way when I joined a local leisure centre, where I was able to swim and do physical exercise in the gym.  Once again I discovered the joy of physical exertion and doing things that contributed to my physical health and wholeness.  I booked a holiday abroad and travelled with a member of my family – enjoying the sights, sounds and smells of a totally different culture.  I found time to play the piano and the guitar and lost myself in making music.  Gradually it seemed that life was taking on meaning and purpose again.

In the autumn of that year I met my second wife, Jean, at a circuit weekend at Willersley Castle, Derbyshire.  We talked together for the first time whilst walking through the beautiful Derbyshire countryside and discovered that we had a great deal in common.  I returned from that weekend strangely disturbed – my spirits had been lifted and my heart had been stirred.  I was now driven by the first compulsive stirrings of love and longed to be reunited with this kindred spirit.  Suddenly life seemed to be charged with meaning and potential, and all I could do was to allow myself to be carried along on this wave of emotion.  It now seemed that the most humdrum activities were invested with meaning – it was no longer a chore to wash, shower, eat, dress; they were all part of the process of being alive.

The greatest gift of all was that I could now feel joy; a deep and lasting sense of joy that welled up inside me. The capacity to love had been reawakened by a stranger who had now become a friend and a lover. As I reflect on this transformation from sorrow to joy, I am reminded that the God we worship and love is a God of joy. A God who generously and graciously pours out his Spirit of joy and gladness into our lives; a Spirit who gradually transforms us and expresses herself through fruitfulness. The Apostle Paul says in Galatians 5:22-23:

> But the fruit of the Spirit is love, joy, peace, patience, kindness, goodness, faithfulness, gentleness and self-control.[2]

However, I recognise that sometimes people are precluded from sensing and experiencing this joy because of the nature of their circumstances, and other people find this difficult to understand. In Niall Williams' novel, Tim Magrath is awkward and embarrassed when Philip tries to articulate his grief and his inability to experience joy. In my own personal journey through grief, I know there were times when I found it incredibly difficult to share the joy and gladness of other people.

Because of this, in my pastoral work as a Methodist minister, I found myself drawn to share the experience of many other people who were hurting and broken. I discovered a natural empathy with those who had lost a loved one, and I became a travelling companion on their journey through grief. Sadly the church is not always the most conducive environment in which people can be openly broken on their journey towards wholeness. I have encountered the casualties of church life – people who have not been allowed to express their brokenness and desolation beyond the prescribed and conventional period of mourning.

I can't help feeling that this is rather ironic when death and resurrection are central themes in the Gospel of Jesus Christ which we purport to live and preach.  Reflecting on all of this leaves me wondering how willing we are to accept people's journeys 'from sorrow to joy'?  Are we ready to welcome and affirm people who, for the moment, simply cannot sing:

'Give me joy in my heart, keep me praising'?[3]

1    Niall Williams, *As it is in Heaven,* Picador, 1999, p.17.
2    New International Version.
3    *Hymns & Psalms* 492, Methodist Publishing House.

I am God's child. He is with me.
So,
Everything in me that is sad is being
    comforted:
Everything that is hurt is being healed:
Everything in me that is crooked is being
    made straight:
Everything in me that is tired is being
    rested:
Everything in me that is good is being
    strengthened.

Margaret Cropper

The fruit of the Spirit comes without effort in the Spirit-possessed soul. Love in service to God; joy in the knowledge of salvation; peace because bitterness is banished from heart and mind; patience, gentleness, goodness and faith.

Anonymous

The fruit of the Spirit are what we *are*. We have no choice about bearing all the fruit or living out the virtues. Our new spiritual nature as Christians is to be loving through the attributes of joy, peace, patience, kindness, goodness, faithfulness, gentleness and self-control. We cannot choose between the fruit we want and do not want to produce. The nature of our new humanity in Christ is to bear all the fruit.

Charles V. Bryant

Later the soul will bring forth fruit exactly in the measure in which the inner life is developed in it. If there is no inner life, however great may be the zeal, the high intention, the hard work, no fruit will come forth; it is like a spring that would give out sanctity to others but cannot, having none to give; one can only give that which one has. It is in solitude, in that lonely life alone with God, in profound recollection of soul, in forgetfulness of all created things, that God gives himself to the soul that thus gives itself whole and entire to him.

Charles de Foucauld

*I need wide spaces in my heart*
*Where faith and I can go apart*
*And grow serene.*
*Life gets so choked by busy living,*
*Kindness so lost in fussy giving*
*That Love slips by unseen.*

*Anonymous*

Consecration is not wrapping one's self in a holy web in the sanctuary and then coming forth after prayer and twilight meditation and saying, 'There, now I am consecrated.' Consecration is going out into the world where God Almighty is and using every power for his glory. It is taking all advantages as trust funds – as confidential debts owed to God. It is simply dedicating one's life, in its whole flow, to God's service.

Henry Ward Beecher

*Holiness and happiness are not two distinct things, but two several notions of one and the same thing.*

*John Smith*

... She took a vow to love. Millions before her had taken the same simple vow but she was different from the majority because she kept her vow, kept it even after she had discovered the cost of simplicity... At some point along the way, she did not know where because the change came so slowly and gradually, she realised that he had got her and got everything. His love held and illumined every human being for whom she was concerned, and whom she served, with the profound compassion which was their need and right ... She could not take her eyes from the incredible glory of his love. As far as it was possible for a human being in this world she had turned from herself. She could say, 'I have been turned', and did not know how very few can speak these words with truth.

Elizabeth Goudge

The Christian faith does not rest on the assurance of any inner person. It does not rest on the assurance of any external authority . . . it rests on the coming to us of the Holy Spirit from without, and meeting the uprising of our Spirit from within, and the result is utter conviction, knowledge, assurance, that we are his children; and it issues in all those glorious fruits in life – love, joy, peace, long-suffering, righteousness – whereby its reality is proved again and again.

Benjamin Drewery

It has encouraged and renewed my ministry to see how the Holy Spirit will work through us if we let him fill our lives. There is a new realisation that God is 'real', an assurance of the indwelling and presence of the Spirit, a renewed sense of the presence of God in our lives. If he could and would do *this* in our midst he can and will do *other things* he has promised.

K. G. Egertson

# Take time to grow

# Steve Cullis

Nothing travels faster than light. In fact light travels at such a tremendous speed that the time it takes for light to travel from a light bulb that you have just switched on to your eye is so quick that the effect of it is instantaneous. If light leaves an object such as a star, in one year the light will travel nearly ten trillion kilometres. All that considered, when you go out at night and see the stars, the light you see from our nearest star, which is called Alpha Centauri, is already about four years and four months old. It took four years and four months for you to see the light you witness tonight to reach here from Alpha Centauri. The light from some of the more distant stars which are visible to the naked eye takes over four hundred million years to travel to your eyes. The light you will see tonight left those stars when the rocks on Greenland were being formed!

Most things that are worth it take time. It took millions of years to form the splendour which we see every time we look up into the night sky. It took generations, not years, to build each of Britain's medieval cathedrals. It takes time for the person who has just put on their L-plates to take their driving test. It even takes time for the young child who has just picked up a violin for the first time to become the mature Yehudi Menuhin. It takes time for the tree to grow. It takes time to wait for the blossom to come, and the fruit to ripen.

Paul picked the word 'fruit' to describe the work of the Spirit deliberately. Even in the world of pre-packaged, supermarket Britain – where strawberries are available from January to December, where 'more' is better but 'instant' is best – growing fruit is never the work of a moment. Even in the world of 'instant' scratch-card wins, 'buy now, pay later' and 'hurry, hurry, hurry to the sales', time remains of the essence if you want to grow fruit. That is true of any kind of fruit: Passion fruit or Love, Avocado or Kindness, Oranges or Joy, Apples or Goodness. Qualities like love, joy, peace, patience, kindness, goodness, faithfulness, humility and self-control are the works of a lifetime. They are never won as a rollover jackpot on a Saturday night.

When you try and express 'love' and forgive someone, you are mostly entering into a lifetime covenant with God. The easy part of forgiveness is when it touches those you love in the first place. Arguments are quickly forgotten. Minor wounds quickly heal. But to those who have hurt you terribly, or those to whom love is not your natural attitude, then the fruit of forgiveness in love is never one instantly achieved. It is usually never a matter of forgiving someone, and that being the end of it. It is most often a case of forgiving each time the memory comes back, letting the hurt go each time you meet that person again. It can be the work of a lifetime, but the completed product is more awe-inspiring than a cathedral and endures into eternity.

When you ask God to make you a kinder person, again the easy part is to be kind to those deserving of kindness. It is easy to be kind to the long-suffering, the generous and the gentle. The hard part of kindness comes when we try to be like our heavenly Father who causes rain to fall on evil and good alike. Kindness is like rain in a hot country in that it softens those who have become hard, and lifts the spirits of those who have become weary. The knack is to spread kindness in the same way as rain falls all too often in this country: indiscriminately and in bulk! The hard part of trying to let the fruit of kindness grow up within ourselves is when we decide that a person deserves not even pity, let alone kindness, and yet we know that we are still commanded to show kindness to that individual. It takes practice, it takes time. It means persevering when you are fed up, and enduring when you have failed. Like any fruit, it seems a long time ripening. Yet the result is more wonderful in God's eyes than all the stars in the universe, and its fruit more enduring than the galaxies themselves.

When we commit our lives to Jesus Christ we are giving God eternity to work with us. When we give ourselves over to God for the first time the whole orientation of our personality is turned around. The intention is there to become a different person – to become like Jesus Christ. In fact, if you look at the list of the fruits of the Spirit which Paul sets out in Galatians, they pretty much describe Jesus' personality. He was kind, gentle, loving, humble, faithful and self-controlled. However, the intention to change and the actual completion of that change are different things. When a super-tanker changes direction, it can take a quarter of a mile from the beginning to the end of the turn. For us, repentance is the recognition that we need to make a U-turn. The growth of the fruits of the spirit in us is the actual 'turn' itself. Whenever you made your commitment to Jesus Christ, you started a process that God, by his Holy Spirit, will complete in you. Don't give up if you feel that that process seems a long time coming – just concentrate on being a more loving person than you were last year. Or, if you will forgive the phrase and not think it too fruity, slightly 'riper' this year than last year!

Four years and four months ago light left the star called Alpha Centauri. If you are awake to see it tonight, your eyes will be sure to see that light. God's work in you is even surer than your eyes are to see that light, and what he has begun, he will surely complete.

*Peace is the gift that comes to those*
*Who, mid life's turmoil, keep their faith serene,*
*And while hemmed in with this world's claims*
*Still hold to things unseen.*

*Peace is not something waiting anywhere,*
*It is the perfect blessing Christ imparts,*
*When self cast out, we have made room for him*
*Within our hearts.*

*Anonymous*

When the truth shines out in the soul, and the soul sees itself in the truth, there is nothing brighter than that light or more impressive than that testimony. And when the splendour of this beauty fills the entire heart, it naturally becomes visible, just as a lamp under a bowl or a light in darkness are not there to be hidden. Shining out like rays upon the body, it makes a mirror of itself so that its beauty appears in a person's every action, speech, looks, movements and smile.

St. Bernard

The more our thoughts and deeds mirror the glory of God as we see it in Christ Jesus, the more we ourselves shall be changed by the Spirit.

Anonymous

*Till your spirit filleth the whole world, and the stars are your jewels; till you are as familiar with the ways of God in all ages as with your walk and table: till you are intimately acquainted with that shady nothing out of which the world was made: till you love people so as to desire their happiness, with a thirst equal to the zeal of your own; till you delight in God for being good to all: you never enjoy the world.*

*Thomas Traherne*

Deep in our nature God's secret ministries are at work, like the mystic power that makes a seed grow, and it will be well if we remember that God is far more eager and constant in his desire for perfection in us than we have ever been.

Leslie Weatherhead

The life of spiritual beauty requires time and variety of experience before it reveals its full authentic self. The soul may gain its vision through sight of Christ's grace in another life, or in a moment of unpredictable and inexplicable illumination; the attainment is spread out over succeeding years, and in different circumstances, some favourable, some adverse. Character never thrives on monotonous ease.

Harold S. Darby

God's grace is richer than prayer. God always gives more than he is asked. Faith is the foundation and basis of prayer: the foundation of faith is the promise of God.

Lancelot Andrewes

All our experiences provide fertile ground for God to plant seeds of faith and bring forth new fruit. Our growth with God, in turn, becomes ministry to others. We see this clearly in the examples of Peter and Paul. From their own failings came insights on the importance and focus of their ministry. We are like them. Our prayer life and spiritual growth will lead us to a greater understanding of our role in ministering to others, whether it be in our families, our work, our neighbourhood, or the wider world.

Ron DelBene

Our world is rife with messages and signatures of the Spirit. Our encounters with one another are potential sites of the awakening and energising that characterise the Spirit. But so much goes unnoticed. We fail so often to recognise the light that shines through the tiny chinks and the dusty panes of our daily lives. We are too busy to name the event that is blessed in its ordinariness, holy in its uniqueness, and grace-filled in its underlying challenge.

Joan Puls

*In ordinary life the unexpected 'rainbow' moments are very special. We hear of some kindness done, enjoy an occasion of fun and laughter, find moments of peace in the midst of a busy life, catch the look on a child's face, visit an old person and come away humbled and grateful for a glimpse of their serenity and courage. But such moments do not last any more than rainbows last and once we have 'traced the rainbow' we have to be prepared to let it go without losing the momentary glory it brought with it. The ability to 'see rainbow colours caught up in the sun' is itself a mark of grace. It is an indication that we have begun to recognise the eternal love and friendship of God reflected in our human relationships in many different ways, transforming them and filling them with hope and love and with unlimited potential for good and for delight.*

*Ann Bird*

## Giving and Taking

Take as a gift
A love all freely given.
A great Lord commends your thrift.
Keep as his gift
This hope of heaven.

To take is hard
For minds narrowed by living.
But open your breath to a word.
To take is hard
When it is giving.

Let breath increase
Within your heart and spirit.
Your gain is his, his gain your lease
Of breath's increase
That gives life credit.

Faith is his bond
Love's capital assures.
Such grace does more than lend.
Faith is your bond.
Give.  It is yours.

Give as a gift
A love all freely given.
A great word reveals its drift.
Treasure the gift
Of spendthrift heaven.

James Kirkup

# Character

# The Harvest of the Spirit

# Roland Bamford

A couple of years ago I enrolled for a computer course at the local college. With the other students I sweated over all the wonders of the modern computer: databases, spreadsheets, all the intricacies of Word and, of course, e-mails and the Internet. The lecturer is so impressed with my progress that she has promised that next term she'll actually let me turn the machine on. Unfortunately, unlike the other students, my problems begin before I leave home. I say to Glennys, my kind and organised wife, 'Remind me what I need, love.' Then together we work through the list: cap, in case it rains, notebook, floppy disk, pencil etc. Even then I sometimes arrive without my banana to eat with my sandwiches, which isn't a disaster because I can buy one at college, or my computer glasses, which is a disaster because I can't see a thing without them and have to trek back home for them.

It's very easy to see the fruits of the Spirit as a list, and to do a check on them from time to time. Can't you see Mr Churchgoer saying to himself as he sets off to work in the morning, 'I've got my discipline, got my joy, got my goodness', then realising halfway through the morning he's forgotten his humility? You can't! No, neither can I, and if he did he'd be wrong.

He'd be wrong because they aren't the *fruits* of the Spirit, they are *the fruit*. They belong together. Together they are the gift of the Spirit to those who live in Christ. Perhaps we get nearer to Paul's meaning when we call them collectively the harvest of the Spirit. They are the different aspects of the life of Christ in us. I love the story of the schoolboy who was doing his RE exam. One question was 'List and explain the Ten Commandments. Only four need be attempted.' For the serious Christian that isn't an option either with the Ten Commandments, or with the harvest of the Spirit. If we are seriously living the Christian life, all the fruit of the Spirit should be beginning to appear in us.

The second fact about the harvest of the Spirit is that it is a gift. It is the fruit of the living Christ living in us. It is the outward sign of a life surrendered to him and to his will and purpose. But although it is a gift, we are called to play our part in making the harvest of the Spirit real in our lives. You must know the lovely legend about the man who went into a shop marked 'The Fruit of the Spirit'. He said to the angel serving behind the counter, 'I'll take one pound of goodness, please, and two pounds of kindness, and as I'm feeling particularly lazy, three pounds of discipline.' The angel replied, 'Sorry, I don't sell the fruit, only the seed.' It is only as we obey the Spirit and allow him to take over more of our lives that the signs of his presence in us grow.

Thirdly, the harvest of the Spirit is not given to us to make us more holy, but more useful. It is eminently practical. As someone in a church meeting once said, 'When all is said and done, much more is said than done.' Or as Florence Allshorn once said, 'A truth isn't a truth until it comes out of our fingertips.' The harvest of the Spirit grows and deepens in us as we use it, share it and give it away. As we hold it to ourselves it withers and dies. It's a bit like Jesus' parable of the talents, when he taught us that what we don't use we lose. Someone once pointed out that, although the water in the Sea of Galilee is fresh and life-sustaining, the water in the Dead Sea is stagnant, and yet the river Jordan flows into both. The difference is that it flows out of the Sea of Galilee again. We go to church for different reasons, sometimes because we are lonely, sometimes because we can see no purpose in life, sometimes because we feel unimportant in the world and want somewhere where we *do* matter. But in the end there are only two valid reasons for worship: the first is to glorify and learn more of the God who has revealed himself to us as Father, Son and Holy Spirit; the second is to line ourselves up with his will. Anything else that worship gives us – peace of mind, meaning in life – is a by-product.

I read the other day about a woman who went on a First-Aid course. Some weeks later her friend asked her if the course had proved useful. 'Yes,' she said, 'very useful. Only last week I was walking down the high street when I heard a terrific crash. Rounding a corner I found a car wrapped round a lamp-post and the driver covered in blood. My knees went limp and for a moment I didn't know what to do. Then I remembered my First-Aid training. I bent down, put my head between my knees and took deep breaths. And it worked; I didn't faint!' That woman had completely misunderstood the purpose of her First-Aid classes, which wasn't to enable her to cope with the sight of blood, but to make her of more use to other people in need.

That is also the purpose of the harvest of the Spirit; God's gift of himself dwelling in us.

*I was baptised with the Holy Ghost and with fire, and felt that perfect love casteth out fear . . . From this time I went forth in the power and spirit of Love. I felt nothing but Love, and desired nothing more but Love . . .*

*John Oliver, in 1762*

If the Holy Spirit has shed abroad the Love of God in our hearts, the fruit of the Spirit will appear in its many forms, and the new commandment of Christ; the only one that he bequeathed to us as the fulfilment of the whole law – Love – will become a reality to us.

Anonymous

*I believe that life is given us so we may grow in love, and I believe that God is in me as the sun is in the colour and fragrance of a flower – the Light in my darkness, the Voice in my silence.*

*Helen Keller*

A loving heart is the beginning of all knowledge.

Thomas Carlyle

Love is the goal.  Love is the way we wend.
Love is our perfect parallel unending line,
Whose only perfect parallel is Christ,
Beginning not begun, End without end:
For he who hath the heart of God sufficed
Can satisfy all hearts – yea, thine and mine.

Christina Rossetti

Take from us, O God, all tediousness of spirit, all
importance and unquietness.  Let us possess ourselves in
patience, and resign our souls and bodies into thy hands.

Jeremy Taylor

I have no desire for wealth, position or honour.  Nor do I
desire even heaven.  But I do need him who has made my
heart heaven.

Sadhu Sundar Singh

*Love is the first and the last and the strongest bond in
experience.  It conquers distance, outlives all changes, bears the
strain of the most diverse opinions.*

*John Watson*

O God of love, we pray thee to give us love:
Love in our thinking, love in our speaking,
Love in our doing, and love in the hidden places
    of our souls;
Love of our neighbours near and far;
Love of our friends, old and new;
Love of those with whom we find it hard to bear,
And love of those who find it hard to bear with us;
Love of those with whom we work,
And love of those with whom we take our ease;
Love in joy, love in sorrow;
Love in life and love in death;
That so at length we may be worthy to dwell with thee,
Who art eternal love.

William Temple

. . . Love is caught, not taught.  One heart burning with love sets another on fire.  The church was built on love; it proves what love can do.

Frank C. Laubach

The root of the matter is a very simple and old-fashioned thing, a thing so simple that I am almost ashamed to mention it, for fear of the derisive smile with which wise cynics will greet my words.  The thing I mean – please forgive me for mentioning it – is love, Christian love.

Bertrand Russell

Praise God for love!
> for love which turns us to one another
> to look with surprise into the eyes of a different face
> and to see who belongs to us.

Praise God for love!
> for love which draws us together,
> out of strangeness and indifference,
> to find friendship and union.

Praise God for love!
> for love which touches us from God,
> reaching across the divide, defying the distance,
> bringing us close, uniting us to God.

Michael Durber

> All loves should be simply stepping-stones to the love of God. So it was with me; and blessed be his name for his great goodness and mercy.
>
> Plato

Love is not a levelling: love meets everyone as the person he or she is and takes them seriously in their particular being.

Emil Brunner

God of the pilgrim way
travel with us on our journey;
be with us at every turn of the road,
draw us ever closer to you.
Make glad our hearts with the radiance of your love;
nurture our understanding of your faithfulness,
that our security may be only in your goodness and mercy,
through Jesus Christ our Lord.

Christine Walters

*Love is the doorway through which the human soul
passes from selfishness to service, and from solitude to
kinship with all humankind.*

*Anonymous*

*Love must be learned and learned again and again;
there is no end to it.*

*Katherine Anne Porter*

Bless me, O God, with the love of thee, and of my
neighbour. Give me peace of conscience, the command of
my affections; and for the rest thy will be done. O King of
peace, keep us in love and charity.

Thomas Wilson

# An Interview
# with Commissioner Alex Hughes
# The Salvation Army

**Should we talk about the 'fruits' of the Spirit, or the 'fruit'?**

Definitely the fruit. I think of a garden when I think of the fruit of the Holy Spirit, with a flower here and a flower there, which together make the whole garden look beautiful. Although you talk about different aspects of the fruit, it is really *the* fruit. The work of the Spirit is eminently practical, and the fruit has to be credible for other people to see – in love, faith, joy and so on.

**How do people receive it?**

The Holy Spirit comes to us in our conversion to Christianity, but there is a difference between *receiving* the Holy Spirit and *being full of it*. We need to be asking God for it all the time. Obviously we have to meet the conditions – God's not going to fill us with the Holy Spirit if there are other things occupying the spaces in our lives, so those things have to go. And in the measure that we're full of the Spirit, I think those gifts – and the different aspects of the fruit – are given to us and they have to be developed.

**How do we do that?**

You can't see an increase in the fruit of the Spirit in yourself, you need your neighbour to see it in you. But the challenge is to be sure that the different aspects of the fruit are increasing in us each day; for example, that people are seeing more love in us. Love has to be obvious in our dealings with people, in the way we speak and act, the way we help people, encourage them, give them dignity. My own personal feeling is that love is the unifying factor in all the fruit of the Spirit; it's the bond that unifies everything else. It's difficult to have patience, for example, unless you love people. It's difficult to have self-control unless you love God and people. It's difficult to have self-control unless you love people and you're willing to make and keep commitments. So the different aspects of the fruit of the Spirit have to be obvious and evident to people around us. I can't say, 'This is my testimony and *I* have love, joy, patience and peace' – people around us have to give their testimony, and I also think that God gives *his* testimony in our lives.

God does something that we can't do for ourselves – he saves us and then empowers us. But that doesn't release us from working with him, making sure that the fruit of the Spirit, the works, are directed towards people. We're not saved by works, but we are saved *to* work for God.

**In other words, it's not about having 'good' feelings of patience, peace and so on, if we don't take them to other people.**

No. If we link the fruit to the Sermon on the Mount we realise that Christianity isn't just about us enjoying life, it's about translating our beliefs into action with people.

**The Salvation Army is best known for that.**

Yes, it is, but we need to keep a balance; that, though we serve people, we don't forget that the best service we can give people is to bring them in touch with God, so they will develop a personal relationship with him. We don't do our work because of that, but if we give a cup of water to somebody we do it in the spirit of Christ, with the prayer that the person will see Christ in us.

Love isn't love until you give it away. And in the Sermon on the Mount Jesus talks about peace, but he says, 'Blessed are the peacemakers', not those who sit back and say, 'I'm so peaceful.' He says, 'Get out into the world where the conflicts are and bring peace.'

You can't divorce Christianity from society, it's a part of it. We're supposed to be the salt of the earth, and people are going to say to us, 'Are you actually *being* the salt of the earth; are you mixing with people, are you having a positive Christian influence; are you bringing that joy, that peace, that patience – are you bringing that to the world in which you live? To the government that governs you? Are you speaking about those issues?'

**Is the fruit of the Spirit something we can be aware of in daily life, to think about each day?**

Yes, we need a quiet time each day to be with God and let his Word speak to us. Then we can move into the day with the Holy Spirit, almost unconsciously asking that the fruit of the Spirit should be present with us. There's a verse in *The Message* paraphrase version of the Bible which sums this up, at the end of Galatians 5. It says: 'Since this is the kind of life we have chosen, the life of the Spirit, let us make sure that we do not just hold it as an idea in our heads or a sentiment in our hearts but work out its implications in every detail of our lives. That means [and this is the verse] we will not compare ourselves with each other as if one of us was better and another worse – we have far more interesting things to do with our lives. Each one of us is an original.' It was that phrase that caught my eye: 'Each one of us is an original.' To come back to the gardening analogy, every garden is an original. The garden's the design of the gardener, and as Chief Gardener God treats us all differently, and helps us to develop the fruit in our lives.

You see some beautiful gardens and you see some others that aren't very beautiful. I remember the old story about a gardener working in a garden and somebody came by and said, 'God made a beautiful job of that garden, didn't he?' and the gardener looked up and said, 'Yes, and you should have seen it when he was looking after it himself!' So we come back to the thought that God doesn't do it all himself, but empowers us to work and co-operate with him. That's why we begin the day asking God for the fruit to become a reality in our lives.

**Have you been aware of the fruit of the Spirit influencing actions in your own life?**

In my ministry I have to deal a lot with people, and perhaps one of the areas where I've really had to depend on the Holy Spirit is when I've had to discipline someone. Of course, the temptation is to rest heavily on the law and judgement, and it's then I've felt the Holy Spirit saying, 'No, that's not the way. It's love, it's grace that's needed. Remember how I dealt with you.' Another area is in trying to bring people the joy of the Spirit – I often hear people being so negative and pessimistic. The joy of the Lord is our strength, and when we lose the joy we lose part of the fruit of the Spirit; we become weaker and more vulnerable.

I think there's a constant call from God for us to cultivate and develop the fruit of the Spirit in our lives. And that means coming before him, before his Word, sharing with others, opening up to him and allowing him to say, 'Look, there's a weed growing there, let's pull it out. Or you have to let me pull it out, because it's inhibiting your growth.' Fruit is about growth, about development.

**Do you get discouraged because the different aspects of the fruit are not especially well-regarded in society?**

It's a normal reaction. If you get someone just *talking* about love, people may listen, but if you get someone *showing* love by going out into the streets, or to one of the stations in London, trying to help young people who come down to London looking for life, only to discover it gets them into drugs and prostitution, then someone looks at that and says, 'Now that I can understand.' Remember they say that a picture's worth a thousand words.

People who see that may not choose your way, but they would have to recognise that that person is showing love to another person. It always comes down to the fact that the one-to-one approach is the best way to spread the Gospel. Rallies, services and so on all contribute, but the most effective way to bring people to Christ is on the one-to-one basis; if you can win your neighbour, win your friend. It's not because of what you've said but because of what you've done.

I like the line from Charley Brown: 'I love humanity, it's people I can't stand!' God tells us to love the person next to us, our neighbour. Christ invariably tells us to make sure that people see him in us. If there's somebody without clothes, somebody who's hungry, or thirsty, or in gaol, then show your Christianity practically.

**Can the fruit wither and die if we don't keep trying to develop it?**

You only have to look at a garden – if it isn't cultivated and cared for it dies. It might go on for a while but eventually it will die. I think that we may not give the fruit the opportunity to develop, and I think God must be disappointed by that. If there's no room for development the fruit doesn't grow, and if a muscle doesn't grow then eventually it cannot be used. The fruit of the Spirit needs to be developed *and* used.

But, on the other hand, if it *is* used, it can bring us great joy. Sometimes a person might say to you: 'You showed real patience, real self-control in that situation', which shows an answer to something you might have prayed about. Or sometimes in prayer the Lord will say, 'We did well there, didn't we? You let me give you what you needed.'

*Take joy home,*
*And make a place in thy great heart for her,*
*And give her time to grow, and cherish her,*
*Then will she come and oft will sing to thee*
*When thou art working in the furrows, ay,*
*Or weeding in the sacred hour of dawn.*
*It is a comely fashion to be glad;*
*Joy is the grace we say to God.*

*Jean Ingelow*

Christ is the source of joy to people in the sense in which he is the source of rest. His people share his life, and therefore share its consequences, and one of these is joy. Partly that is to say, joy lies in mere constant living in Christ's presence, with all that that implies of peace, of shelter, and of love.

Henry Drummond

Joy is for all people. It does not depend on circumstance or condition; if it did, it could only be for the few. It is not the fruit of good luck, or of fortune, or even of outward success, which all men cannot have. It is of the soul, or the soul's character; it is the wealth of the soul's whole being when it is filled with the spirit of Jesus, which is the spirit of eternal love.

Horace Bushnell

That his prayer was nothing else but a sense of the presence of God, his soul being at that time insensible to everything but divine love; and that when the appointed times of prayer were past, he found no difference, because he still continued with God, praising and blessing him with all his might, so that he passed his life in continual joy; yet hoped that God would give him somewhat to suffer when he should grow stronger.

Brother Lawrence

Abide in the Father's love by spiritual joy. Joy is love flaming. One saith that laughter is the dance of the spirits, their freest motion in harmony, and that the light of the heavens is the laughter of angels. Spiritual laughter is the laughter of the Divine love, of the eternal Spirit which is in our spirits.

Peter Sterry

In every life which is working harmoniously there will be the strong impress of Joy, as the fruit of the Spirit growing up in the soul which is alive to God.

W. C. E. Newbolt

Once, I remember, as I was coming home over the rise above the village, the houses below, and the familiar fields, suddenly became incredibly beautiful. They were no different to what they had been before, and yet they were different. *Joy burned in them.* The sun had set and the trees stood out, sketched with swift black strokes on an orange sky. The great dome of air was swept, and clean. Elation rushed up inside me, as if a barrier had suddenly given way before it.

Richard Hillyer

... Every day my sense of joy
Grows more acute; my soul (intensified
By power and insight) more enlarged, more keen.

For thence we have discovered ('tis no dream –
We know this, which we had not else perceived)
That there's a world of capability
For joy, spread round about us, meant for us,
Inviting us.

Robert Browning

We must be joyful now. Here . . . within . . . with who we are and what we've got.

Tim Hansel

Joy seems so much more vital and contagious than anything else I know. Joy means victory, discovery of God for yourself, which is the only real knowledge we ever get, and which spurs us on for another new world to conquer.

Jean Bolton

*The God who had such heart for us*
*as made him leave his house*
*come down through the archipelagos*
*of stars and live with us*
*has such a store of joys laid down*
*their savours will not sour:*
*the cool gold wines of Paradise*
*the bread of heaven's flour.*

*He'll meet the soul which comes in love*
*and deal it joy on joy*
*as once he dealt out star on star*
*to garrison the sky;*
*to stand there over rains and snows*
*and deck the dark of night;*
*so God will deal the soul, like stars*
*delight upon delight.*

*Robert Farren*

True joy is a serene and sober motion . . . the seat of it is within, and there is no cheerfulness like the resolution of a brave mind.

Seneca

Here morning in the ploughman's songs is met
    Ere yet one footstep shows in all the sky,
And twilight in the east, a doubt as yet,
    Shows not her sleeve of grey to know her by.
Woke early, I arose and thought that first
    In winter-time of all the world was I.
The old owls might have halloed if they durst
    But joy just then was up and whistled by
A merry tune which I had known full long,
    But could not to my memory wake it back,
Until the ploughman changed it to the song.
    O happiness, how simple is thy track!
– Tinged like the willow shoots, the east's young brow
    Glows red and finds thee singing at the plough.

John Clare


Life is a pure flame, and we live by an invisible sun within us.

Thomas Browne


O God great and wonderful, who has created the heavens, dwelling in light and beauty, who has made the earth, revealing yourself in every flower that opens; let not my eyes be blind to you, neither let my heart be dead, but teach me to praise you even as the lark which offers her song at daybreak.

St Isidore (adapted)

# Making Holy Ground

# R. A. Henderson

Most of us, at one time or another, have probably hankered after the more heroic brand of Christianity. Perhaps we wouldn't go so far as St. Teresa of Avila, the great Spanish mystic, who, as a child, did her level best to run away from home to be a martyr, taking along her reluctant small brother. Nevertheless, some sort of grand gesture (and the general acclaim that goes with it) would appeal to the self-image of many people.

It's discouraging, then, to look at St. Paul's list of the 'fruits of the spirit' and see that there's little evidence of heroism there. Oh, of course, it's admirable to be loving and joyful, peaceful and patient, kind and faithful and gentle. But it's not very exciting (indeed, it sits oddly with what we know of Paul's own fiery temperament); it smacks of the old 'Gentle Jesus meek and mild' image which has long gone out of fashion. And as for the last item in Paul's catalogue: self-control . . . well, it's all very British (stiff upper lip and all that), but we know that there's a rich vein of emotion in many people: think of the outpouring of grief, complete with sentimental gestures – flowers and teddy bears – over the death of Diana, Princess of Wales. It really seemed as though the British had abandoned their traditional phlegm, and comment on this phenomenon was largely positive. At last, our notorious reserve was under attack.

Is this, then, what I can expect if I really open myself to the Spirit? Doesn't it sound rather boring? Where are the agony and the ecstasy? Come on, Lord: *self-control?*

As a translator, I know how easily meaning can slip away in the transfer, however conscientiously carried out, from one language to another. Translations of the Greek word that lies behind 'self-control' vary: temperance, says one version, choosing a term which for many readers may call up unfortunate associations with a campaign against over-indulgence in alcohol; self-mastery, says another, in close correspondence with the usual term in my second language, Italian, *dominio di sé*. This looks more interesting: the self as a wild beast that must be mastered.

But perhaps we need to rethink our idea of 'self-control' in any case. We tend to define it in negative terms – not crying in public, not losing your temper, not making a display of emotion; but all of this can just as readily be expressed in more positive language, as peacefulness, patience, kindness and gentleness: Paul's 'fruits of the Spirit' in fact. Nor should we be too ready to underestimate the cost of self-control: from the mother who, with an effort, refrains from smacking her howling toddler as she drags him round the supermarket, to the international politician who chooses to negotiate rather than go to war, at every level of public and private life we are called on to exercise self-control day by day. From this point of view, it's clearly a fruit to be cultivated assiduously, in the interests of the community – whether that community be the family home or the world stage; and as such, a challenge and a focus for our energies.

Yet the other 'fruits of the Spirit' remain obstinately ordinary: even passive. They are exactly the virtues that characterised my mother, and, I suspect, a great many other mothers: women whose family was their life, who never so much as thought of battling for any kind of supremacy. I'd even go so far as to say that they are traditionally feminine virtues, with their emphasis on submission and rejection of dominance – except of that unruly self which is so often in conflict with the Spirit. This is not to say that I am advocating (or that I believe the Spirit is advocating) a return to the days when a woman's place was, ineluctably and unchangeably, in the home: as a professional woman myself, it would ill behove me to suggest any such thing. It remains true, however, that the spirit of what in Italian is called *oblatività* – altruism, self-sacrifice – typically associated with women, can transform conflict into fruitful collaboration. Certainly the confrontational style of many activist groups, in defence of the environment, of animals, of particular ethnic or social groups (immigrants, gays, battered wives or whatever) achieves little, and may even provoke further hostility. The exercise of patience, gentleness and kindness would probably be more productive: small virtues, in the sense that they make no allowance for any tendency to histrionics, offer no opportunity for striking attitudes; domestic virtues, to be practised in the context of the most ordinary of lives, in our dealings with family, neighbours, colleagues and friends.

And that, of course, is the point. Just as Jesus himself started his public ministry in intensely local, unspectacular circumstances – healing a friend's mother-in-law who had a bit of a temperature, saving a bride and groom from social embarrassment when the wine ran out during the wedding celebrations – so we, with the help of the Spirit, can make 'holy ground' of our own immediate vicinity.

During the Second World War, in Amsterdam, a young Jewish woman, Etty Hillesum, kept a diary in which she recorded her discovery of God. It is an extraordinary account of those very 'fruits of the Spirit' Paul writes about. Through her increasingly generous, self-giving love for a man with whom she had an often troubled relationship, this young woman came to a realisation of the presence of God in her life: 'Deep, deep within me there is a well. And in that well is God.' For her, as for the Samaritan woman in the Gospel, the 'living water' was there to be drawn up and transform her. Her love for a single individual, too, was radically changed by her love for God: 'My being is transforming itself,' she wrote, 'into a single, great prayer for him. And why just for him?

Why not for others too?' Letters and recollections of her behaviour in the concentration camp where she died testify to the growth, in Etty Hillesum, of the fruits of the Spirit, without in any way diminishing the sense of a strong, independent personality. So it would seem that there is no reason to fear that the fruits of the Spirit will suffocate our individuality, or that being gentle, patient, kind and faithful will compromise our moral or emotional energy.

I have to admit that I have more trouble with joy! Certainly if I give myself wholeheartedly in the service of God, my satisfaction, at the deepest level, will be complete. The trouble is that serving God doesn't preclude suffering, and never has; and we are – or at least *I* am – too weak to embrace suffering with the unreserved, holy joy of self-immolation. Yet its attractions are clear. 'Joy', obviously, in this context, doesn't mean the permanent grin of the complacent, or the thoughtless cheerfulness of the 'I'm all right, Jack' mentality. Rather, it is the corollary of love, which finds fulfilment not in self-gratification but in the gift of self to the beloved. We can all experience this, in a small way, when we give up some personal satisfaction for the sake of someone we love: parent, offspring, spouse or friend. It may cost us a good deal, but the pain of self-denial is outweighed by the joy of knowing that we have contributed to the well-being of the beloved. And when the beloved is God, our joy in giving is complete.

It all comes back to love, the first item on Paul's list – the first, because it is pre-eminent, the necessary condition of all the rest. To love is to put the other (or the Other) above self, unreservedly, constantly, at whatever cost. Perhaps in those terms we can call it heroic after all.

Peace is like gossamer –
vulnerable, yet indestructible:
tear it, and it will be rewoven.
Peace does not despair.
Begin to weave a web of peace:
start in the centre
and make peace with yourself
and your God.
Take the thread outwards
and build peace within your family, your
    community
– and in the circle of those you find it hard to like.
Then stretch your concern
into all the world.
Weave a web of peace
and do not despair.
Love is the warp in the fabric of life:
truth is the weft:
care and integrity together –
vulnerable,
but ultimately
indestructible.
Together,
they spell
peace . . .

Kate Compston

I am a man of peace. I believe in peace. But I do not want peace at any price. I do not want the peace that you find in stone; I do not want the peace that you find in the grave; but I do want the peace which you find embedded in the human heart, which is exposed to the arrows of the whole world, but which is protected from all harm by the power of Almighty God.

Mahatma Gandhi

*Serenity is distinctive and divine. There is a peace of God, a peace of Christ, a peace of the Spirit, all one divine peace . . . This serenity is not idleness, nor stillness, nor is it the boon of a life that is remote from care, dwelling in some dream island to which the wings of a dove carry the wistful heart; it is peace in the midst of care, the fruit of the Spirit in an atmosphere that may be hostile rather than kind to such fruitfulness . . . It means that the central citadel of life is guarded by the divine Spirit, kept by a control that will never give way. However much the storms of life and circumstances may beat and blow upon the surface, the deep inwardness of life retains its untroubled calm.*

*John Macbeath*

There is no really true joy except in some measure a spiritual satisfaction of the soul is found in the knowledge, love and service of the Lord.

W. L. Watkinson

## Before Daylight

Enter into the stillness of the dawn,
the stillness that waits
below the surface of the hour's business,
the eternal quiet welling
beneath the pounded pavement of the world's road.

Enter in
not to escape the trouble
but to draw living strength
to give yourself to each face, each task, each moment.

Enter the pool of presence.
Draw peace there, to be peace
in the garden of the given day.

Julie M. Hulme

*Peace is not the absence of conflict from life, but the ability to cope with it.*

*Anonymous*

Let there be love and understanding among us;
let peace and friendship be our shelter from life's storms.
Eternal God, help us to walk with good companions,
to live with hope in our hearts and eternity in our
thoughts,
that we may lie down in peace and rise up
to find our hearts waiting to do your will.  Amen.

Jewish prayer

Do we fail to be anxious for nothing, and to bring everything by prayer and supplication with thanksgiving before God? We may bring nine difficulties out of ten to him, and try to manage the tenth ourselves, and that one little difficulty, like a small leak that runs the vessel dry, is fatal to the whole. Like a small breach in a city wall, it gives entrance to the power of the foe. But if we fulfil the conditions. he is certainly faithful, and instead of our having to keep our hearts and minds – our affections and thoughts – we shall find them kept for us. The peace which we can neither make nor keep will itself, as a garrison, keep and protect us, and the cares and worries which strive to enter in vain.

Hudson Taylor

*O God our heavenly Father, keep us from all nastiness of temper and from all lack of thought for others in little things. Teach us to be patient with those whom we cannot understand, to be loving towards those who depend on us. For Christ's sake. Amen.*

W. J. May

The exercise of patience involves a continual practice of the presence of God.

F. W. Faber

O God, my Father, give me patience all through today.
Give me patience with my work, so that I may work at a
job until I finish it or get it right, no matter how difficult or
boring it may be.
Give me patience with people, so that I will not become
irritated or annoyed, and so that I may never lose my
temper with them.
Give me patience with life, so that I may not give up hope
when hopes are long in coming true; so that I may accept
disappointment without bitterness and delay without
complaint.
Hear this my morning prayer for your love's sake.

William Barclay


One immediate fruit of patience is peace, a sweet
tranquillity of mind; a serenity of spirit, which can never
be found unless patience reigns. And this peace often rises
into joy.

John Wesley


*Take out of my life, dear Lord, all fret and
hardness. Make me calm, quiet and courageous.
Put music into my voice and sunny graciousness
into my manner, for Christ's sake.*

*Anonymous*

# Tropical Fruit

## Jill Baker

I once attempted to count the number of black, glossy seeds contained within one pawpaw . . . I must admit I gave up when it became clear that the total would be more than a thousand! We were living in Grenada at the time, a small island in the South Caribbean where my husband, Andrew, and I were Mission Partners with the Methodist Church there. The pawpaw in question was not home-grown but one of many we were given over our eight years in the Caribbean, time spent more or less equally between St. Vincent and Grenada. Another incalculable figure would be the quantity of fruit we were given by church members and neighbours during those years. I didn't keep a record, but without doubt it would run into dozens of breadfruit, water melons and pumpkins; hundreds of passion fruit, grapefruit and pineapples, and thousands of bananas, mangoes and oranges! Generosity, Galatians 5:22 (NRSV) tells us, is itself a fruit, a fruit of the Spirit, and this generosity was as abundant in those fertile lands as the very fruits themselves! Indeed, fruit and generosity seem to go hand in hand, and it is remarkable what can spring from such a combination – soon after we had moved to Grenada I answered the telephone to hear a woman's voice say, 'You don't know me, but I grow a lot of limes, would you like some?' Of course I said yes, and that was the start of an unexpected but enduring friendship.

Harvest festivals, in such an environment, were in quite a different league from the tastefully arranged pyramids of canned and packaged food, interspersed with the occasional basket of shop-bought fruit or eccentrically-shaped home-grown marrows which I recall from my suburban childhood! The churches and chapels of these rural, West Indian villages would be literally full to overflowing – sugar cane formed into arches at the entrances and standing ten feet tall in great bundles in every corner, the Communion rail completely hidden behind festoons of sweet peppers, passion fruit and oranges still on their branches with leaves attached; whole bunches of bananas and plantains in all their confusing (to an Englishwoman) varieties stacked in every available space, heaps of yams, sweet potatoes and every fruit and vegetable known in the land. I remember the first harvest festival we celebrated in Chateaubelair, St. Vincent; our younger son had just begun to crawl . . . what fun would he have, what chaos would he wreak amongst all these goodies? As it happened, the first thing he laid hands on was a prickly pineapple, with its sharply serrated leaves still intact . . . he kept away after that and, for once, stayed quietly in our pew!

Fruit formed a very large part of our lives in the tropics. In Chateaubelair hardly a day went by without a caller at the manse bringing something from their garden. I must admit that in the height of the mango season this could become too much of a good thing – I well remember a morning spent literally up to my elbows in mango pulp (and 'plenty mangoes' means 'plenty flies'!) making mango juice, mango ice cream, mango sorbet, even mango bread (not a success), anything to use up the bounty. As I washed the last sticky drops of juice from my hands and the kitchen, Andrew returned from a morning's pastoral work, bearing several large carrier bags of mangoes . . . just for a moment I did cynically wonder if the widow of Zarephath ever became tired of oil and flour! Of course, in the hot, sticky tropical climate, fruit was a blessing; when we first arrived – constantly thirsty – I was impressed by the ingenuity of the local folk who could turn any fruit into a delicious refreshing drink. Soon I learned to do the same and our thirsty English guests could be revived with passion fruit juice, lime squash, or (although I never really mastered this one) soursop drink, made from the delicious, almost yoghurt-like white flesh of a large, knobbly green fruit.

But let us return to that pawpaw (not the mini-versions sometimes available in UK supermarkets, but something considerably larger than a rugby ball) – the health-giving, mineral-packed orange flesh is sliced open and the peppery black seeds (also good to eat themselves) are revealed and I muse, 'Is each one of those little seeds really capable of producing a pawpaw tree which, if it doesn't fall victim to a disease descriptively known as "spongey top" [as ours inevitably did] may itself bear over its life span many dozens of similar fruit, each one containing yet more innumerable seeds?' Theoretically, yes! What an amazing act of generosity on God's part to give each pawpaw tree so many, many chances to reproduce itself.

I feel sure that Paul chooses fruit to illustrate these Christian virtues quite deliberately. For the quality that defines what is a fruit is its ability to bear within itself the seeds of its own reproduction. The core of just one apple can give rise to many, many thousands of apples; one mango stone might grow into a huge tree, producing myriads of mangoes. This pattern applies just as much to the fruit of the Spirit, which we are called to bear as Christians. We all know this to be true in our own experience, that love breeds more love, that peace spawns further peace, that joy gives birth to greater joy. We have perhaps read of the habit of one of our earlier Methodist saints who, if confronted by a rude or ungracious waitress or shop assistant would see it as a personal challenge, a challenge to the life of the Spirit bearing fruit within him, to win the person over, with kind words, smiles, attention, goodness. As fruit of the Spirit, love and kindness, when demonstrated in real-life everyday situations carry within themselves the seeds of a potential explosion of love and kindness!

We could all give many examples; stand with me at the back of a smart new office, recently opened in Kingstown, the capital of St. Vincent, as the trading centre for a new cable TV company. We are revisiting the island on holiday and are waiting to exchange a few words with one of the staff, a young woman who went through the youth group in Chateaubelair in our time there. However, it is a busy afternoon and customers keep claiming her attention, so we stand aside and wait. It seems that all the customers have one thing in common – they are all angry. The cable TV company is clearly still experiencing teething problems – there have been breaks in transmission, delays in repairs, people feel they are not getting their money's worth, and all the rage and frustration of these dissatisfied customers is being unleashed upon our innocent friend! Somehow – by God's grace – she remains serene; she listens respectfully to each complaint, allowing the fury to be spent and adding no fuel to the fire with self-justification or excuses for her employers; she continues to smile calmly, she apologises, she promises that the matter will be looked into. By her active demonstration of the Spirit at work in her life, producing patience, gentleness and self-control in the face of irritation, harsh words and loss of control, the fruit which is so evident in her own life begins to cast its seeds into other people's lives and they go away, to some extent at least, soothed.

'I hate people who sing in the mornings,' Snoopy complains. Perhaps we sympathise, and yet we also acknowledge that pure, holy joy is infectious – as a fruit it carries within itself the possibility of endless reproduction. All parents know that displaying the fruit of the Spirit in our dealings with our children yields a plentiful harvest – the more patience we show, the more patience they learn and demonstrate themselves, the more they meet faithfulness in their family life, the better they will be able to form faithful relationships and so on – not that it's always easy! Sometimes we seem to be so short of these essential fruit; we live with our spiritual fruit bowls empty or perhaps containing one shrivelled up apple, and one or two softening pears! We scrape around to find enough love to speak civilly to our neighbour, enough peace not to feel stressed-out by coffee-time every day, enough joy to smile at those we meet in the street and in the shops. Even in church we can be sadly lacking in these same virtues – and when love is missing from our fellowship, when joy is absent from our worship and when peace is a stranger to our business meetings, then the harvest we reap as congregations is meagre and we will see little growth or sign of new life. How can this be when our God is the great gardener himself, the one who provides seed extravagantly and who himself gives 'water springing up to eternal life' (John 4:14)?

In Chateaubelair, St. Vincent and in St. George's, Grenada, our 'fruit bowl' was a huge, locally made wicker basket and even that was usually too small – at Christmas time, especially, boxes would line the kitchen filled to overflowing with every variety of fruit in its season – tangible evidence of the abundance of *spiritual* fruit in the hearts of our congregations. For in the Caribbean we also encountered a rich harvest of love in action, joy in worship, peace and contentment in living and a never-failing generosity, even the poorest of our church members would share what little they had with us and with others – a humbling experience.

Jesus, too, talks about fruit; three times in Matthew's Gospel (7:16; 7:20 and 12:33) he says that we will be known by our fruit. This is an acid test which challenges men and women in every sector of society; politicians are renowned for their promises – but by their fruits you shall know them; millionaires put their confidence in their bank statements – but by their fruits you shall know them; film stars, singers, models take every possible care with their appearance – but by their fruits you shall know them. Many of us, perhaps, would rather Jesus had said we would be known by our words – it's often easy to say the right thing – or by our church attendance, or by our business successes or social contacts . . . but by our *fruits* we shall be known in a world thirsty for the refreshing taste of love, joy, peace, patience, kindness, generosity, faithfulness, gentleness and self-control.

*A wise rabbi was walking down a road when he saw a man planting a tree. The rabbi asked him, 'How many years will it take for this tree to bear fruit. The man answered that it would take seventy years. The rabbi asked, 'Are you so fit and strong that you expect to live that long and eat of its fruit?' The man answered, 'I found a fruitful world because my forefathers planted for me. So I will do the same for my children.'*

*The Talmud*

Let us worship God.  In worship we behold the goodness of God, and become partakers of that goodness; in worship we see the patience of God and become partakers of that patience; we celebrate the purpose of God and offer ourselves as servants of that purpose.

Nels Farré

*Grant unto us, Almighty God, that when our vision fails, and our understanding is darkened; when the ways of life seem hard, and the brightness of life is gone, to us grant the wisdom that deepens faith when the sight is dim, and enlarges trust when the understanding is not clear.*

*George Dawson*

Give me, O Lord, purity of lips, a clean and innocent heart, and rectitude of action. Give me humility, patience, abstinence, chastity, prudence, justice, fortitude, temperance. Give me the spirit of wisdom and understanding, the spirit of counsel and strength, the spirit of knowledge and godliness, and of thy fear. Make me ever to seek thy face with all my heart, all my soul, all my mind; grant me to have a contrite and humbled heart in thy presence – to prefer nothing to thy love.

A Gallican Sacramentary

Let your baptism serve as a shield, your faith as a helmet, your love as a spear, your endurance as full armour. So be patient with one another in gentleness, as God is with you.

Ignatius

Spirit of endless compassion,
your care for us
is the support that all carers need,
to transform weariness into patience,
and patience into hope.
Come with strength and joy.

Bernard Thorogood

Kindness, loving kindness, motivated by my love, is a mark of my grace in you. Be kind to one another and let others show kindness to you.

I am kind to you all without favour or reserve. My wonderful kindness to you is like the blue of a fair day, like the soft rain in the growing season. It is the touch of one who loves you, the smile of one who cares for you.

In my kindness there is nothing violent, nothing abrasive, but I give out my kindness with openhanded gentleness.

Kindness is at first in your hearts, then in your words and deeds. Be kind to one another. Be open to give and receive kindness.

Judith Pinhey


One kind word can warm three winter months.

Japanese proverb


Kindness is the art of making the other person as happy as you would like to be yourself. It is not the whim of a sentimentalist but the pattern of good living.

Anonymous

Without love and kindness, life is cold, selfish and uninteresting, and finally leads to a distaste for everything. With kindness the difficult becomes easy; the obscure clear; life assumes a charm and its miseries are softened. If we knew the power of kindness, we should transform this world into a paradise.

Charles Wagner

*Let us remind ourselves over and over again that holiness has to do with very ordinary things: truthfulness, courtesy, kindness, gentleness, consideration for others, honesty and courage in the face of life, reliability, dutifulness.*

*Ruth Burrows*

Think deeply, speak gently, love much, laugh often, work hard, give freely, pray earnestly and be kind.

Sue Ryder

*The ministry of kindness is a ministry which may be achieved by all people, rich and poor, learned and illiterate. Brilliance of mind and capacity for deep thinking have rendered great service to humanity, but by themselves they are impotent to dry a tear or mend a broken heart.*

*Anonymous*

Kindness is the golden chain by which society is bound together.

Goethe

*Gracious and holy affections have their exercise and fruit in Christian practice.*

*Jonathan Edwards*

Cheerfulness means a contented spirit, it means a pure heart, it means a kind, loving disposition, it means humility and charity.

W. M. Thackeray

# The Birds and the Bees?

## Maureen Henderson

Fruits only form when the flowers have been fertilised by bees, butterflies or other insects which visit the flowers for their tempting nectar. I remember hearing a preacher say that the fruits of the Spirit have to grow in our lives – too many of us are running around with cut flowers!

Consider what will enable those fruits to form and grow. As the fruits of the earth need the right conditions to come to fruition, so do the fruits of the Spirit. What is the equivalent of good fertile soil, adequate sun and rain, protection from frost and damaging winds for the nourishment of the fruits of the Spirit? Here the comparison is relevant since different plants need varying conditions. You won't get apples in tropical Africa but there are many other luscious fruits there which won't grow in England, even in hothouses. You only have to see the wizened little pawpaws in the tropical house at Kew to realise that.

So our first requirement is to be ourselves. That is the greatest gift God has given to each one of us – and to the world! Does that make you sit up? In a retreat address a few years ago I heard a sentence I have never forgotten: 'You are your particular shape of God's love in the world.' This startling statement is true since each one of us is unique and has been put on this earth by God to live out our particular vocation.

Our primary vocation is to be human, and Jesus has shown us what it means to be truly human. The trouble with many religious people is that they try to be too good before they have learnt to be human – hence they rush around with bunches of cut flowers, wearying themselves and other people. I have long thought that religion should come with a health warning: THIS COULD SERIOUSLY DAMAGE YOUR HUMANITY! Perhaps religion is better used like a condiment – very sparingly.

One Pentecost I came across the words 'Learn to live and move in the Spirit.' Those words struck me very forcibly and led me to pray for grace to know their meaning. A short time later the penny dropped. The first lesson (and the second and the third) is to RELAX. Relax and be yourself. Religious people do have a tendency to be very earnest, and to try to be other than themselves, often attempting to model themselves on some saint and hero. Good role models can be helpful but there is a danger of ending up discouraged. There is too much copying going on. We need to have the courage to live our own lives. I believe that is the meaning of obedience: especially learning to develop the neglected, unused parts of ourselves.

Traditionally we talk about the nine fruits of the Spirit listed in Galatians 5:22-23: love, joy, peace, patience, kindness, generosity, faithfulness, gentleness and self-control, but the word fruit is singular. The virtues listed there all come together as a result of living life in the Spirit. So I feel at liberty to add a tenth – a sense of humour!

I lived for thirty years in a Religious Order under a strict Rule, but the one bit I really did appreciate was: 'They will value highly a sense of humour and mirth.' Life in community is impossible without a sense of humour. I believe Jesus had a wonderful sense of humour (he was Jewish, after all). It comes out in his teaching, and without it the tax collectors and outcasts of society wouldn't have enjoyed his company so much.

If we were to relax and not take ourselves so seriously we would be much easier people to live with. So many of our relationship difficulties arise from stress and tension. We can't have a stress-free life. It wouldn't be desirable, we'd end up like jellyfish! However, we could save ourselves a lot of stress if we slowed down and took time to 'consider the lilies'. That involves swimming against the tide of our culture and so requires discipline. Not many of us can have a lot of time for prayer and reflection but we can all take minute vacations – to consider the miracle of growth in the trees and flowers we pass, or even just the grass or weeds growing through the flagstones. I've even seen mushrooms pushing their way up through tarmac. Those short moments can restore perspective to our lives. There is more to life than our personal problems.

So relaxing and taking ourselves less seriously can be important early steps for mission. The Gospel is good news where we are. We can hardly proclaim the Gospel if our lives are harassed and heavy. What we are speaks more loudly than what we say.

I have a friend, Fiona, who loves life. At the age of eighty she is still very energetic, though she admits to running out of energy more easily these days. She has a large family and very many friends. She worries about her relative wealth but is so generous with her hospitality. She frequently drives people to hospital and other appointments (a real sacrifice of time) and is the sort of person you feel better for meeting in the course of your day. She never hides the fact that she is a Christian yet she worries that she is not spreading the Gospel. 'I'm no good at talking about it,' she says, unaware that who she is tells its own story. The fruits of the Spirit just flow from her and she seems totally unaware of the fact. Her enjoyment of life is infectious.

Enjoyment is so important as it is a cleansing and liberating thing. If we enjoy people we will accept them as they are and not try to change them. We will enjoy their individuality and particular gifts and be tolerant of their faults and foibles. Enjoyment liberates us from trying to improve people and do good to them. (How I hate being done good to!)

It is that unselfconscious flow of the fruits of the Spirit, rooted in a knowledge of God's love and the validity of our particular experience of that love, which the world needs so much. For most of us this will be lived out in very local and humdrum ways that may appear to us to be unimportant. But this is the 'seed growing secretly' in our own lives and those around us. I am convinced that God's most important work is hidden from our eyes – better that way, we are less likely to spoil it.

One of the most misunderstood fruits of the Spirit is peace. All too often the idea of peace means 'a quiet life for me'. That is not the peace which Jesus offers. Rather it can mean disturbance of my long-held cherished views of myself and the world. It can propel me out of my comfortable armchair into struggle and conflict, into finding the courage I didn't know I had, into confronting and campaigning against injustice, local or global. The life of the Spirit does not lead us to a sweet and tranquil life. It leads us to co-operation with our neighbours, of all faiths and none, to help create a better world. We will make new friends, discover other world views and see the same Spirit at work in those who belong to very different cultures and backgrounds. Through that we will discover the rich kaleidoscope of God's world and rejoice to have our place in it.

Although no longer living in a multi-ethnic neighbourhood I keep in contact with my friends from other faith traditions, I simply can't live a full and creative life without them. One of my Muslim friends often telephones or visits me. He has been having a very difficult time recently; he shares his difficulties with me and asks for my prayers. He went on pilgrimage to Mecca and brought me back three traditional gifts – a Muslim rosary, a packet of dates and some perfume. The prophet Mohammed broke his fast with dates at the end of a day in Ramadan, so that continues to be the custom for Muslims during Ramadan. These dates from Medina were particularly good since they were stuffed with almonds. There is a Hadith or teaching of Mohammed that encourages the application of perfume before coming to prayer, a delightful reminder about preparation for prayer.

I was so moved by these presents as an expression of the warmth and richness of our sharing and friendship. We do have marked differences in our belief and practice but the same Spirit unites us and enriches our humanity. Being human is wonderful. Jesus has shown us that, and calls us to be human rather than religious. Rooted in being human together in God's wonderful world our flowers will be fertilised and so bear fruit.

*Where there is charity and wisdom,*
*there is neither fear nor ignorance.*
*Where there is patience and humility,*
*there is neither anger nor disturbance.*
*Where there is poverty with joy,*
*there is neither covetousness nor avarice.*
*Where there is inner peace and meditation,*
*there is neither anxiousness nor dissipation.*
*Where there is fear of the Lord to guard the house,*
*there the enemy cannot gain entry.*
*Where there is mercy and discernment,*
*there is neither excess nor hardness of heart.*

*Francis and Clare*


Grant me, O Lord, to know what I ought to know,
to love what I ought to love,
to praise what is precious in thy sight,
to hate what is offensive to thee.
Do not suffer me to judge according to the sight of my
    eyes,
nor to pass sentence according to the hearing of the ears of
ignorant men;
but to discern with a true judgement between things
visible and spiritual,
and above all, always to inquire what is the good pleasure
of thy will.

Thomas à Kempis

*Character*

To solve the human equation, we need to add love, subtract hate, multiply good, and divide between truth and error.

Janet T. Coleman

All progress is made by people of faith who believe in what is right, and, what is more important, actually do what is right in their own private affairs.  You cannot add to the peace and goodwill of the world if you fail to create an atmosphere of harmony and love right where you live and work.

Thomas Dreier

I prefer a firm religious faith to every other blessing.  For it makes a discipline of goodness; creates new hopes, when those of the world vanish.

Humphrey Davy

105

O God, in whose hands lies the destiny of all your children, do not forsake us when the years take their toll of our minds and bodies . . . keep your Spirit blowing around and within Us. Maintain us confidently in Christian hope, resolute in the faith and worthy always of your love.

Vera Dowie

Happy is the people whose God the Lord is: for all things shall work together for their good. They may sit secure in exercising faith upon God, come what will. They have ground for prayer, for God is a prayer-hearing God, and will be inquired of by his people as to all their concerns in the world. And they have ground for the greatest encouragement and comfort amidst all the events of providence, seeing they are managed by their covenant God and gracious friend, who will never neglect or overlook his dear people, and whatever concerns them.

Thomas Boston

God calls me to be faithful, not successful. The end result is in his hands, not mine.

Charles Colson

We do not understand
Joy until we face sorrow
Faith until it is tested
Peace until faced with conflict
Trust until we are betrayed
Love until it is lost
Hope until confronted with doubts.

Source unknown

Life has no question that faith cannot answer.

Thomas l. Johns

*Without faith we are as stained glass windows
in the dark.*

*Anonymous*

The life of faith is not a life of mounting up with wings, but
a life of walking and not fainting. Faith never knows
where it is being led, but it loves and knows the One who
is leading.

Oswald Chambers

*Faith ought to be tried and tested, if it be faith. I don't like that faith which is a 'precious, tender plant', to be sedulously guarded under a glass cover, or in a hothouse – but it is a tough principle within us, bearing heavy weights and hard work, or it is worth very little.*

*John Henry Newman*

If your faith in God is stronger for every humble task in which you need and get his aid, then that humble task is necessary to the fullness of your faith in God. It will make the music of your life more firm and solid.

Phillips Brooks

As the flower is before the fruit, so is faith before good works.

Richard Whately

*We strive for righteousness and truth and faith, and the Holy Spirit is there to help us. He gives us strength for the weary day, guidance in time of confusion and sustaining grace for every need.*

*Kenneth E. Roach*

# Waiting to Grow

## Elizabeth Canham

In our back garden at home it was a challenge to find enough fertile soil in which to grow spring flowers. One year, when I was about six years old, I was given a tiny plot and a packet of marigold seeds. My mother helped me turn the soil, make a hole for each seed and then smooth over the earth and water it. I was excited by the prospect of an abundance of the orange flowers illustrated on the seed packet. A day later I went to investigate my flower garden; nothing there. For several days there was sharp disappointment as I ran to look for evidence that my marigolds were growing. Finally I could bear it no longer and began to dig in the soil to uncover the all-too-slowly-germinating seeds. Over the next weeks, I dug in the flower bed, uncovering and replanting the seeds each time. I think that by summer, two of the marigolds had managed to survive and bloom on weak looking stalks!

Today I know the wisdom of Jesus' words, 'unless a grain of wheat falls into the earth and dies, it remains just a single grain; but if it dies, it bears much fruit' (John 12:24). The seed needs undisturbed time, gestation time, in which to prepare for the season of fruit. Hidden in the darkness it slowly develops, absorbs nutrients and must wait for sun and warmth to wake it when winter is over. What is true for seeds applies to disciples of Christ also. We must often wait, sometimes in what seems like impenetrable darkness, to discern God's way for our lives. And for many of us waiting is not easy; patience is one of those fruits of the Spirit that elude us and we keep digging up possibilities that preclude healthy growth. The key to harvest is allowing time to run its course.

By nature I am impatient – still like the six year old – and I live in a culture which colludes with my desire for instant response to wants. Perhaps this is why I have been especially blessed when others have gifted me with their time and taught me to slow down. Several years ago I was besieged by endless media requests for interviews following my controversial ordination in the USA. Early one morning after I had met with a group of priests on a return visit to England and celebrated a Communion service one of them invited me to accompany him on a short walk to his parish church near St Paul's Cathedral. When we arrived he suggested that we go downstairs into the ancient crypt. It was a sparsely furnished space with an altar, crucifix and a few chairs. We sat together on the front row and I waited for the expected questions or requests. None came. Time passed and as the silence continued I realised that I was being given a gentle and much-needed gift. Time to be, to let go, to cease my attempts at being superwoman and instead receive the gracious offering of time and presence from this caring fellow Christian. Tears came to my eyes as I realised how much I needed these moments of quiet waiting and I sensed that God smiled when I finally stopped the frenetic pace that had sapped my energy.

Gestation is of vital importance in the life of the Spirit. I need to schedule times of intentional retreat when I leave routines and busyness in order to become more available to God. These are not always 'burning bush' experiences. It takes *time* to slow down, *time* to catch up on sleep, and *time* mixed with a generous dose of patience when confusion, distraction or boredom seem to be the order of the day. Out of time spent alone with God comes an awareness of the importance of offering to others not just a superficial greeting but a presence which lets them know that they are valued. I cannot be on permanent retreat, but I can choose time each morning to be in quietness, reading Scripture, waiting for God's Word to feed my spirit and make me more alert to opportunities for showing love, joy, peace, patience, kindness, generosity, faithfulness, gentleness, self-control.

Recently I bought a new dishwasher and the owner of the local appliance store came to install it on a Saturday morning. It should have been a simple matter to remove my old dishwasher and replace it with the new one. This was not the case. After struggling for more than an hour and a half, the old appliance remained firmly stuck in place, wedged in by a complicated series of copper pipes. I had met the store owner several months earlier when he came to repair my oven, and had learned then that he was a new Christian, deeply devoted to his Bible and studying New Testament Greek in order to understand it better. His face shone with joy when he spoke of how his life had been changed through faith in Christ and now I was to see how he lived the Gospel. Although his store closed at noon, he went on working through the afternoon, making two trips to the hardware store for replacement pipes and screws, patiently dealing with the many problems caused by earlier unprofessional plumbing. The fruit of the Spirit was evident in this man, not primarily in what he said, but in the quality of patient attention he brought to his work.

Many years ago, at the beginning of a long retreat, my spiritual director handed me a poem by Jesuit writer Pierre Teilhard de Chardin. It began with the advice: 'Above all, trust in the slow work of God', and went on to name our impatience at being on the way to the unknown. Our ideas mature gradually and we need to let them grow, to shape themselves without undue haste. De Chardin encourages us not to force them on 'as though you could be today what time . . . will make you tomorrow'. 'Don't keep digging up the seeds,' he seems to imply, 'let them gradually take in what time alone can give them to become healthy fruitful plants.' My spiritual director had wisely assessed my great desire for clarity, an experience of the holy and longing for a 'quick fix' and called upon me to trust in the slow work of God.

The message about waiting for God's time is often present in Scripture. The Bible also tells us that God waits for us to be ready – for *kairos*, or the right moment to act. It was 'in the fullness of time' that God took flesh in the body of Mary, a young peasant woman, in order that we might no longer be bound by laws but welcomed by grace into the family of God as beloved children. I hear God address me through Scripture – 'Be still and know that I am God'; 'Rest in the Lord and wait patiently' – but I heard the same message clearly some years back through the words of a South Carolina Highway Patrol Officer. I had been stopped for speeding along a narrow, two-lane road during the peach picking season when the normal fifty-five mph had been reduced to accommodate truckers conveying the fruit. I was penitent, embarrassed and profoundly relieved when, instead of issuing me with a speeding ticket, the officer gave me a verbal warning. As I returned to my car and was closing the door he called out to me, 'Ms Canham, SLOW DOWN.' I drove the rest of the way home pondering his words, and hearing in them a reminder once again of God's desire for my unhurried presence. For the next week I began each day with my journal, reflecting on ways to be more attentive, more present to each moment, each person, each opportunity to allow patience space to grow.

The poem with which I conclude this article was penned as I watched my cat recovering from surgery. She is incredibly patient, willing to wait for what she needs even when that means being present to painful experience. I honour her for the many lessons she has taught me throughout the fifteen years of our acquaintance:

\* \* \* \* \*

'I haven't got time for the pain,' they say,
a caplet or shrink
will settle everything –
insomnia, neurosis, constipation –
cherry flavoured
oblivion
and a blast of TV
first-aiding the forgetting.

Cats know better.
Attentive to the pain
they wait wide-eyed
and watch.
Curled and still
they let the hurting be
and, wiser than humans,
yield themselves to now.

Pain asks for time,
requests our presence
and teaches us the measure of our joy.
We drink the bitter cup
and angels bear us
through the dark night
of our unknowing
into the Easter moment.

*You can never trust God too much.*
*Why is it that some people do not bear fruit?*
*It is because they have no trust*
*either in God or in themselves.*

Meister Eckhart


Herein for me, is Faith. 'Launch out into the deep,' says Jesus. 'Venture on him, venture wholly,' we used to sing. Granted, we are hazarding everything; there is the risk that we could be wrong. Yet there is so much to fortify us, as we let go, out into the Unknown; so much that says, 'Go on!' There is the Beauty that we find in the world around us. There is the sheer Goodness in people. There is the Joy and Love in human relationships.

David Francis


Let us have faith that right makes might; and in the faith let us dare to our duty as we understand it.

Abraham Lincoln


114

The quiet anger of the meek is a terrible thing. Just because their zeal for righteousness is largely undeflected by our own ceaseless self-reference, they are formidable warriors in the cause of truth. Gentleness is not weakness, but restrained strength.

John Newton

Give us grace and strength to forbear and to persevere.
Give us courage and gaiety and the quiet mind.
Spare to us our friends, soften to us our enemies. Bless us, if it may be, in all our innocent endeavours. If it may not, give us the strength to encounter that which is to come, that we may be brave in peril, constant in tribulation, temperate in wrath, and in all the changes of fortune and down to the gates of death, loyal and loving to one another.

Robert Louis Stevenson

O Lord, this is all my desire – to walk along the path of life, that you have appointed me, even as Jesus my Lord would walk along it, in steadiness of faith, in meekness of spirit, in lowliness of heart, in gentleness of love.

Anonymous

Thank God every morning when you get up, that you have something to do that day which must be done, whether you like it or not. Being forced to work, and forced to do your best, will breed in you temperance and self-control, diligence and strength of will, cheerfulness and content and a hundred virtues which the idle person never knows.

Charles Kingsley

Lord, I my vows to thee renew;
Disperse my sins as morning dew;
Guard my first springs of thought and will
And with thyself my spirit fill.

Direct, control, suggest, this day,
All I design, or do, or say,
That all my powers, with all their might,
In thy sole glory may unite.

Thomas Ken

Temperance is the moderating of one's desires in obedience to reason.

Cicero

When you are in the right, you can afford to keep your temper; and when you are in the wrong, you cannot afford to lose it.

G. I. Lorimer

*Nothing is so strong as gentleness – nothing so loving and gentle as strength.*

*Francis de Sales*

Giver of the increasing good,
take my thanks for all that has made me what I am;
for all my yesterdays, their discipline, their pleasant songs,
my unanswered prayers,
even for those whelming hours in which
I have seen how frail I am without thee.
And when the morrow comes,
with a new duty or a new truth,
may the door of my mind be open,
and I at the door bid them welcome.

Alistair MacLean

# Miracle of Grace

# Denis Duncan

'The harvest of the Spirit' is the wonderful, evocative phrase used in William Barclay's translation of the New Testament to describe, in St. Paul's letter to the Galatians (5:22), what the Authorised Version calls 'the fruit of the Spirit'. The harvest of the Spirit is 'love, joy, peace, patience, kindness, goodness, fidelity, gentleness and self-control'. All these qualities are the product of the life which is nourished by the Spirit. They are gifts of grace. We reap what the Spirit has sown.

It was the aim of Paul's letter to establish clearly the essential message of the Gospel which is that 'No one can get into a right relationship with God by means of doing the things that the law prescribes. The only way to get into a right relationship with God is through faith in Jesus Christ' (2:16). We are not saved by works but by grace. It is by faith alone that we are 'justified'. 'In Christ's school we are made right with God through faith' (3:24).

The doctrine of justification by faith lies at the heart of our belief about how we attain to life. 'Salvation by works' is a counsel of despair. Salvation by faith is a counsel of hope. The harvest of the Spirit is not the merit through which we achieve salvation. It is the product of the salvation which we have, in grace, been given.

'If the Spirit is the ruling principle of our lives we must march in step with the Spirit' (5:25). 'Growth in grace and the likeness of Christ' will develop slowly but surely until we reap the harvest of the Spirit and begin to produce the fruit that bears testimony to the miracle that has taken place within us.

'I am not going to treat the grace of God as if it did not exist,' Paul declares (2:21). What a striking statement that is! It comes (as most of the New Testament quotations in this article do) in William Barclay's translation and is made with real emphasis. Its effect must have been dramatic then. It remains so today. We cannot hope to produce the harvest of the Spirit unless the grace of God *is* real and *felt to be real*. When that happens, the road to the development of the fruit of the Spirit is open.

The evolution of love, joy and peace and their associated qualities is not a task of will. It happens only as 'grace abounding' is present in the deep places. We cannot resolve to have 'the harvest of the Spirit'. We can, through grace, create the possibility of producing such fruit. It comes not through resolution but dedication, by keeping in touch with the Spirit. It is not effort but gracious acceptance of a gift which makes the harvest possible. It is not the flow of our adrenaline that leads to good works. It is the divine flow of love within us.

This is the miracle of grace. The harvest will come not because we resolve, but because we receive; not because we set ourselves moral standards but because we ask for and are given the grace that brings a spiritual quality of life; not because we increase our 'good works' target but because we allow the Spirit to flow through us in abundance.

> My will is not my own
> till thou hast made it thine.
> If it would reach a monarch's throne
> it must its crown resign.

So George Matheson, in his hymn 'Make me a captive, Lord', encapsulates the paradox that is, in human terms, foolishness, but in divine terms, faith triumphant. The only way to life is through death. The only way to victory is through surrender. The only way to resurrection is through the cross. It is, I repeat, a miracle of grace. Only if the seed is put into the ground and it dies, Jesus told us, can it bring forth the harvest.

> And from the ground there blossoms red
> life that shall endless be

as Matheson wrote in his hymn, 'O love that wilt not let me go'.

Traditionally, on entering into full membership of the church, there are vows to be made. The first of these is a confession of faith in Christ, a recognition of the turning point (which 'conversion' means) which is reached when we are restored into that right relationship with God, made possible by the gift of grace. The second is a commitment to 'serve the Lord all the days of life'. This will be expressed in the process of 'maturing into Christ', 'trying', as Paul said to the Philippians, 'to have the same attitude to life as Jesus had' (2:5).

It is in this context (it used to be called 'sanctification') that we are required to make an effort. Discipline is involved. The 'means of grace' – prayer, Bible reading and reflection, participation in worship, receiving the sacraments – have been provided to help us grow in faith. It is, as is particularly true of the season of Lent, a journeying with Jesus that will be expressed in increasing fruits of the Spirit. It is a personal pilgrimage towards wholeness. But the Gospel, though it emphasises personal responsibility, is essentially a corporate experience. So many of the words used in the early church were corporate words – fellowship, community, body. They still are – congregation, church, flock, communion and so on. It is an essential part of mission to try to develop communal fruits of the Spirit too. The mere mention of the first three qualities listed by Paul (love, joy and peace) is enough to make us realise how much these very attitudes need to be cherished by society. There are international, national, local, family situations desperately in need of just these things. The disciple cannot impose these on society, groups or even other individuals. All that can be offered is a personal commitment to produce the harvest of the Spirit by keeping in touch with the Spirit, and hoping something of creative possibility may rub off on our society.

It is important to remember that while every possible form of communication, traditional and modern, should be part of the church's communication, ultimately the most profound and effective method of communication is the witness of 'the holy life'. It is that of which Paul speaks when advising Timothy (2 Timothy 1:9 NIV) how to cope with ministry in a hostile society. The phrase itself may sound somewhat pious to our modern ears, but we know what it means. Did not those who witnessed the healing miracle effected by the disciples in the early church say of the disciples that they demonstrated that 'they had been with Jesus' (Acts 4:13 AV). They would probably have been surprised to learn of the witness they had made quite unaware that they were making it, but such witness is effective. They had unwittingly testified to the one they sought to serve.

Of all the qualities generated by the Spirit, in both the personal and the corporate contexts, love, joy and peace are supremely desirable. Love is the most fundamental of Christian qualities for 'God is love'. It is the basis of 'the golden rule', anchoring religion in the eternal triangle of mutual love between God, human beings and neighbours. It is the quality that is, in the words of William Barclay's translation, 'patient with people, and kind'. There is no envy in love; there are no proud claims; there is no conceit. Love never does the graceless thing; never insists on its own rights: never nurses its wrath to keep it warm. Love finds nothing to be glad about when things go wrong, but is glad when truth is glad. Love can stand any kind of treatment; love's first instinct is to believe in people; love never regards anyone or anything as hopeless; nothing can happen that can break love's spirit. Love lasts for ever. 'Love is of God' so it is the greatest of the fruits of the Spirit. How sorely that love is needed today!

Love is that corpus of outgoing attitudes that evolves from God's love for us. It embraces compassion, empathy, sympathy, acceptance, grace-fullness, concern, forgiveness, understanding and caring. It is God reaching out in welcome, for it is in this way that 'God first loved us'. It is an enabling, not a compelling quality. It is always encouraging, for love does not dominate; it cultivates. Love is service that seeks no return, no thanks, no honour. Love is the tireless touch that tells another: 'I am here.' It is, indeed, the first fruit in the harvest of the Spirit.

Joy is no superficial emotion, no noisy expression of amusement, no passing involvement in pleasurable play. It is a quality of smiling radiance that goes deep into our inner being. It is a profound quality, a product of grace and faith. It reflects the divine joy, so clearly indicated when 'one sinner repents'. In a world of gloom and grim reality, the need for genuine joy is great.

Peace is, the Psalmist says, the recovery of something lost. 'But I will call on the Lord and he will save me,' he writes (Psalm 55:16-18, NEB). 'He has heard my cry . . . and gave me back my peace.' This is a peace the world cannot give. It is the deep peace of reconciliation and relationship restored. Such peace brings true perspective. There is a sustaining strength conveyed by the Spirit that enables serenity and tranquillity to replace fear and anxiety. 'Thou shalt keep him in perfect peace whose mind is stayed on thee' (Isaiah 26:3, AV).

It is a privilege to encounter those in life whose demonstrated love, joy and peace is evidence of the harvest of the Spirit in them. I think of a brief meeting with the noted Japanese Christian, Toyohiko Kagawa, who served the people of Kobe despite his own physical weakness. Or Sister Frances Dominica, that wonderful nun who founded and directs Helen House in Oxford where terminally and seriously ill children and their families are looked after and sustained. Or the late Cardinal Hume, whose simplicity and sincerity – despite his being involved at the highest level with politicians, statesmen and public people – remained obvious. His serenity in the face of coming death was a witness to religious and non-religious alike.

I think, too, of Alida Bosshardt, the Amsterdam Salvation Army officer, who worked for nearly thirty years in the red-light district of her city, friend of the prostitutes, welcome visitor to every pub and club, totally respected representative of the faith to whom, because of her manifestly 'holy life' every door of every kind was open. Words hanging on her study wall testify to her understanding of ministry and her purpose in life:

> The glory of life is to love, not to be loved;
>     to give, not to get
>     to be a strong hand in the dark to another in time of need
>     to be a cup of strength to any soul in a crisis of weakness
> This is to know the glory of life.

The greatest medium of communication remains the holy life, that is a life characterised by the fruit of the Spirit. 'Since we live by the Spirit, let us keep in touch with the Spirit.'

1   This article is based on the section 'The Harvest of the Spirit' in the author's *Creative Silence* (1998).

2   *The New Testament, A Translation* by William Barclay (Arthur James 1998). The phrase 'the harvest of the Spirit' is also used in The New English Bible (OUP 1970). Where 'the fruit of the Spirit' is used, as in the Authorised Version and the New International Version, it is singular, not 'fruits'. The biblical texts quoted are from William Barclay's translation unless otherwise noted.

# In Action

# Keep in Touch

# Richard Chartres

'Since we live by the Spirit, let us keep in touch with the Spirit.'

St. Paul's words came alive for me in an unexpected place. I was visiting a residential centre for people recovering from drug abuse. Residents, who are often referred to the centre on release from prison, stay for an average of four months, trying to get their lives back on track.

I was very nervous as I approached the glass-plated front door. The arrival of a bishop can either immobilise people or they can treat you as a Palladium turn. The warden did not improve matters by pointing out a large man in the lobby and saying, 'That man, bish, has had more convictions than you have got.' That did nothing for my confidence.

It was, however, that very man who, when I had actually come through the door, asked me to sit down and talk with him. There began one of those rare conversations where the defences were down, no one was pretending and we found ourselves speaking heart to heart.

The spiritual atmosphere of the centre depends on a very honest permanent team led by a prayerful Christian. I have only rarely experienced a place where the Holy Spirit was so palpable.

One of the gifts of the Spirit is profound communication. The Spirit opens the channels so that we converse with God and with the spirit in others, heart to heart, subject to subject. That was the experience of the apostles on the day of Pentecost when, although many members of the crowd spoke languages unfamiliar to Peter and the rest, every one could understand the joy and the truth of the communication.

Much of the evil in the world comes from treating other people, and God himself, as objects. We tend to look on the surface of things and say with the wisdom embedded in ordinary speech that we are 'sizing someone up'; 'weighing them up' or, even worse, 'looking down on them'. Information of a kind can be acquired from viewing other people from the outside as objects. Such a viewpoint does not disclose, however, the inside knowledge and compassion which comes when we communicate in the Spirit, heart to heart.

Then there was another remarkable thing about our conversation. Many of us go through life saying, 'I've got a problem, and my problem is you, or the boss, or the government', but the Spirit of truth teaches us that there is no real spiritual progress until we can look inside ourselves, unafraid, and see the shadows that are there in every one of us.

My friend had endured a childhood of abuse and neglect. He told me a couple of stories in a matter of fact way. He could have blamed everyone except himself and he would have had some justification after such a horrendous start in life. In fact he said, 'I've learnt in here that my main problem is me, and if I want change it has got to begin inside.'

The Spirit of compassion gives us the courage to see the shadows within and see through them. If we see through the shadows, we feel pain but it is healing pain. If we cover up and do not face the world inside then the shadows grow in power and can turn us into slaves of some addiction.

The Spirit is always giving us clues about the reality within. For example, one of the laws of the spiritual life is that we most dislike in others things which we suffer from ourselves. Whenever we have a surge of dislike for someone we have just met, we need to hang on to the experience because the Spirit is trying to tell us something about ourselves.

Finally, my friend said that he had already spent nearly four months in the centre and he was due to return home at the end of the week. 'I don't know how I am going to cope back in my old haunts,' he said, 'but I do know that I am stronger. They haven't been soft in here. They have shown me what I have done with my life so far but they have listened as well, and they trust me to change. I feel stronger and worth more than I did four months ago.' The Spirit is a powerful healer and can heal wounds and bind up the broken-hearted. It was no surprise that my friend said that he wanted to stay in touch with the staff who had helped him.

The Spirit relates us profoundly both to God and to the dark continent inside us but the Spirit also relates us to one another in non-lethal relationships which can be healing. Life in the Spirit leads us beyond ourselves, to God the beyond–all. The Spirit can also be experienced within ourselves and relate us to our own spiritual centre but the Spirit also relates us to one another. Spiritual life is between us. The gift of the Spirit came, according to the Acts of the Apostles, 'when they were all together in one place' and the Holy Spirit is a gift to us in the community of faith.

Just before I went to talk with some other residents, my friend said to me, 'I've learnt this. If you wanna stay clean you gotta stay in touch.' It was an eloquent and rhythmic way of paraphrasing St. Paul: 'Since we live by the Spirit, let us keep in touch with the Spirit.'

We could stay in the house of the Lord for ever,
saying our prayers and singing his praises
with people who think as we think coming
to join in the comfort and peace of it all;
to exchange the good news, to glow together
friends among friends, birds of a feather.

But there on the doorstep lies the world,
turbulent, violent, sick and sorry,
full of fierce arguments, weeping and loveless

(nothing like us who are blissful and beaming
singing our hymns in the house of the Lord).

Come, let us open the door and step out
fearlessly into the dreadful confusion
of those who believe what we do not believe,
of those who are seeking and those who are faithless
and those who seem lost to all love for their sins.

Out, out and let us radiantly run
to the stranger, the outcast, the sick unto death,
with our message of healing, our glorious hope,
our truth that turns hate into love,
grief into joy, rain into roses,
ill into well, dross into gold . . .
sharing the fruits that have fed us so often,
here as we sit in the house of the Lord
glowingly saying our prayers together,
friends among satisfied friends,
birds of an unruffled feather.

Virginia Thesiger

It is possible either to sustain and strengthen this burning of the spirit, or to quench it. It is warmed above all by acts of love towards God and our neighbour – this, indeed, is the essence of the spiritual life – by a general fidelity to all God's commandments, with a quiet conscience, by deeds that are pitiless to our own soul and body, and by prayer and thoughts of God.

From *The Art of Prayer*

Comfort the poor, protect and shelter the weak, and with all thy might, right that which is wrong. Then shall the Lord love thee, and God himself shall be thy great reward.

Alfred the Great

O Lord, Spirit of beauty and holiness, dwell within our hearts: that as the disciples were made brave and faithful by thy presence, so may we be filled with the same courage and devotion, and may set ourselves with all thy servants to win the world for Christ.

M. L. Jacks

To the spiritually sensitive, the ordinary happenings of any ordinary day are seen in a special light; as opportunities to receive grace from God and to do his will immediately. When we are spiritually alert, we find that almost every day God is opening doors all round us, doors into new forms and exercises of love, into new opportunities of service, into new spheres of fruitful discipline.

J. Neville Ward

*Fight on, thou brave heart, and falter not, through dark fortune and through bright; the cause thou fightest for, so far as it is true, is very sure of victory.*

*In the long stretch of uneventful days, amid familiar scenes and repeated tasks, amid all the gaining and the giving, all the doing and the bearing, beneath the sky, blue today and grey tomorrow, blessed are the pure in heart, for they shall see the spiritual eventfulness of earth's monotonies, the meaning of its passing services, the glory beneath the dust, the eternal in every hour – and seeing these things is seeing God.*

*Percy Ainsworth*

Teach us, O glorious Lord, to begin our works with fear, to go on with obedience, to finish them in love, and then to wait patiently in hope, and with cheerful confidence to look up to thee, whose promises are faithful and rewards infinite, through Jesus Christ.

Hickes' *Devotions* (1642)

This is our prayer to thee, O Lord; strike, strike
    at the root of penury in our hearts.
Give us the strength lightly to bear our joys and
    sorrows.
Give us the strength to make our love fruitful in
    service.
Give us the strength never to disown the poor
    or bend our knees before insolent might.
Give us the strength to raise our minds high
    above daily trifles.
And give us the strength to surrender our
    strength to thy will with love.

Rabindranath Tagore

Life became an adventure in learning to love . . . I used to
think there was something in me that was too precious to
run the risk of mixing with ugly, ordinary things – a kind
of mystical dream that might grow into something very
beautiful, if I kept my mind up in the clouds enough and
did not allow it to be soiled. And now I know that life is
clean, dirty, ugly – beautiful, wonderful, sordid – and
above all Love. I even used to think I was rather good at
that. I used to think that being nice to people and feeling
nice was loving people. But it isn't, it isn't. Love is the
most immense unselfishness, and it's so big I've never
touched it.

Florence Allshorn

You are the caller
You are the poor
You are the stranger at my door

You are the wanderer
The unfed
You are the homeless
With no bed

You are the man
Driven insane
You are the child
Crying in pain

You are the other who comes to me
If I open to another you're born in me.

David Adam

I want to make the most of whatever light people have got, however slight it may be, to strengthen and deepen whatever they already possess, if I can . . . Christianity taught us to care. Caring is the greatest thing, caring matters most.

Friedrich von Hügel

*Faith and works are like the light and heat of a candle; they cannot be separated. Faith without works is like a bird without wings; though she may hop about on earth, she will never fly to heaven. But when both are joined together, then the soul mounts up to her eternal rest.*

*Joseph Beaumont*

# You cannot 'Catch the Bird of Heaven'

# Michael Begg

It took many years for me to appreciate that I should expect to find the fruits of the Spirit among those who are not within the Christian family. If we are to keep in touch with the Spirit we need to open our eyes to recognise the Spirit's activity in unexpected situations and among people of different faiths.

Many journeys and encounters with Jews, Muslims, Hindus and Buddhists and especially with those who claimed to have given up on religion, have opened my eyes. In places and with people where I had no expectations of an encounter with the divine I found myself standing on holy ground as I experienced something of the power and grace and sign of the kingdom of God.

### Rats and the Angel of Bangkok

The rats and smells encircled us in the slums of Klong Toey as we ate tasty food at a stall in the street. So long as I kept my eyes averted so as not to see the signs of sweated labour, the street children, inhuman living and working conditions, solvent abuse and prostitution and appalling poverty, I could cope with our conversations with those who worked among and with the 'slum people'. They spoke of Melissa, known by the street children as 'our leader', a slight young woman who day by day rounded up the street children in the slums. She washed, fed and talked with them about their lives and families. Most of them had been abandoned by their parents, and she tried to reunite them with their families. She is a familiar and welcome sight in the heartless Samrong district of Bangkok. The children clearly love her and respond to her approach. Melissa herself was a child worker before leaving the factory to work with the church's programme in that area.

Against a background of oppressive illegal working conditions and in defiance of wealthy employers Melissa smiled her way through the streets. Minutes later as we followed, we heard some children shout a greeting to her, this teenager they called the 'Angel of Bangkok'. With infinite patience, love and commitment she stopped and smiled, listened and encouraged the waifs from the street, while she listened to their unbelievable but true stories. Melissa was kindness personified. She was a sign for me of the presence of God's Spirit.

**Antelopes and paradise in Burundi**

'This is paradise,' said one of the hapless 'prisoners' in a cramped concentration camp not far from Bujumbura. 'We have a little food, we have a little medicine, we have a little water. This is paradise.' I did not know what to say.

I met Josephine. 'They hunted us like antelope,' she said as she squatted in the dirt in the shade of a three-sided, dilapidated corrugated frame draped with plastic sheeting. This was home for her family. She recounted the horror and fear as she, her family and thousands of others were hunted down like animals and then transported to the camps. 'I do not want to go back to the hills because we are afraid of being killed. My house was destroyed by fire.'

The men gathered round. They read a list of things they needed in the camp. Josephine simply said, 'I am not asking for your prayers. I have nothing now. Before I had many things. I try to pray. I try to find some work. I hope God will help me.'

Yet again I was lost for words. Changing the subject, as I have so often when embarrassed in awkward or horrifying situations where God was only noticeable by his absence, I asked her the names of her children. In translation the two oldest were called 'God sees me' and 'Thank you'. I had looked in vain for some signs of hope. It was only when I met Josephine that I found God in this hell-hole. In spite of everything she kept faith with God. At the time I would have found it hard to say that God had kept faith with Josephine and her people. But when her youngest two children were born in the camp she named them 'Thank you, God' and 'It is God who sees all things'. She was for me a sign of the kingdom. A sign of the presence of the Spirit of God.

**In a dry and thirsty land**

Four haystacks appeared on the horizon. They were moving towards me across the crusty barren earth. Thousands of cattle and wild animals had died. The reservoirs were dry valleys. Elephants were succumbing; even the donkeys were dying.

Now, on this Saturday morning in Matebeleland after six hours in the bush, Isobel and three friends were returning home, each bearing a huge stack of tinder-dry straw, balanced on their heads, which they had cut from the scorched earth. They were hoping against hope that it would keep their few remaining cattle alive. With their backs straight, they knitted as they walked. When they heard I was a pastor they stopped and with some effort lowered their heavy burdens. In the midday sun their strong voices wafted across the dying land, rebuking my feelings of hopelessness. They sang in harmony Psalm 1. Words of faith and hope, about trees that would bear fruit. I contemplated the dying trees that offered no shade and no hope of life. The women told me that their four children were called 'Strengthen', 'Frighten', 'Obey' and 'Stride On'.

My spine still tingles as I recall that morning. I hear their voices of defiant hope as they strode on, and I hear God's Spirit moving.

**The day God died**

I stood in the church among the bones of some five thousand women and children. The sickly smell of death clung to the walls and pews of the church. The rotting clothing, bedding and cooking utensils bore witness to one of the many genocide sites in Rwanda. 'I died three years ago. I am as the dead, I feel dead. There is no word to say,' said Nsabimana Malk, who kept watch at the church at Ntarama.

He showed me the knife used to finish off a dying woman or child, the bullet holes in the skulls of the fortunate, and the signs of the suffocating fire that eliminated those who had vainly sought refuge in the Sunday school. I walked away and wept in despair. All that I thought I knew and believed, all that had sustained me in many places of suffering and evil evaporated. I was desolate.

I said in a whisper: 'Where was God?' Without hesitation my hired translator, a Tutsi, replied confidently, 'He was in the church.' There was a time when I might have said something like that. I wondered what God was doing in the church.

He must have been bleeding and screaming and suffocating and choking and dying.

For many months anger and compassion and grief overwhelmed me. Faith and hope had almost gone. And

137

then one day I was challenged by the thought that, though I could meet the suffering, hungry, thirsty, naked, imprisoned Christ in other people, I had failed to meet him in my own brokenness.

How much easier it is to discern the signs and the fruits of the Spirit in other people's lives than in our own, just as it is easier to see Christ in other people's suffering and brokenness. My own experience led me eventually to the point where I was able to recognise in my own anger, compassion, love and bereavement echoes or reflections of God's love and compassion. Only then did I begin to find the way towards resurrection, and towards a new way of being a disciple of Christ. Only then did I understand the meaning of a sentence I had often quoted: 'To be a Christian is to have your heart broken by the things that break the heart of God.'

Back in Ireland I began to rediscover what is sometimes called Celtic spirituality. It was something I had known without knowing the name. It was about recognising the signs of the presence of the divine in all things and this has led me along a new path. It is a path where I do not expect God to intervene but one along which I discover God is already journeying.

Avelin, our home and now a centre for Celtic retreats, has welcomed many visitors. Many were on the edge of, or beyond the church. Some claimed to have given up on religion altogether. Yet they displayed, and in some cases rediscovered, those precious fruits which I had only expected to find among Christians. How foolish and blind I had been! It had led to a prejudice which over many years prevented me from welcoming with open arms people of other faiths and many of no faith. I had been blind to the evidence of God's Spirit at work. I believe now that they were people for whom religion no longer gave a language to express their hopes and loves and longings, but they were people in whom the Spirit of God was bearing fruit. They were people not unlike me.

Slowly I began to recognise God within. It was not a comfortable feeling, but it began to ring true. Words of Paul about the Spirit groaning within us, waiting for something to be born, took on new meaning. I recall a song by Sydney Carter which includes words about vain attempts to 'capture the Holy Spirit, the bird of heaven'. I know that the Spirit is free and on whom he will, he bestows his fruits.

I know that you cannot catch the bird.

Peace is not the journey's end
but the journey's making.
It is the struggle to be free,
response to hunger's cry;
walking with the derelict
and hearing the oppressed.

Peace is not idling on still waters
but riding out the storm,
braving the wide ocean,
charting unknown seas,
throwing the life-line to the drowning
from the ship that foundered on the rocks.

Peace is not a dream of unrealised hopes;
it is running for the prize;
it is training to attain,
accepting the cost of following,
being ready for the sacrifice and pain;
it is the faith that dares to find a way.

Peace is not the false prophet's haven of rest.
It is the challenge of the Prince of peace;
the calling from the God of peace;
fruit of abiding in the Spirit of peace.
It is responding to the call of Christ
to announce good news, the gospel of peace.

John Johansen-Berg

*We can do no great things, only small things with
great love.*

*Mother Teresa*

Because of our faith in Christ and in humankind, we must apply our efforts to the construction of a more just and humane world. And I want to declare emphatically: such a world is possible. To create this new society, we must present outstretched, friendly hands, without rancour – even as we show great determination, never wavering in the defence of truth and justice. Because we know that seeds are not sown with clenched fists. To sow we must open our hands.

Adolpho Perez Esquivel
(speaking as he received the Nobel Peace Prize)

God – let me be aware.
Stab my soul fiercely awake with others' pain,
Let me walk seeing horror and stain.
Let my hands, groping, find other hands.
Give me the heart that divines, understands.
Give me the courage, wounded to fight.
Flood me with knowledge, drench me in light.
Please, keep me eager just to do my share.
God – let me be aware.

Miriam Teichner

Make no doubt about it, responsibilities toward other human beings are the greatest blessings God can send us.

Dorothy Dix

The closer we draw to others, the closer we draw to God. When we are willing to abandon ourselves and to fling ourselves outward in compassion and service, we find that we have made room not just for others in our lives but also for God in our hearts. The energy that we had massed in our own little centre is spent on others, leaving an open space where God may enter. From this same God-infused centre also flows the renewing energy that allows us to keep loving and serving in the world.

Thomas R. Hawkins

To be persons, in the Christian sense, means that we must bear one another's burdens. We must be prepared to suffer pain for one another and to carry each other in love through times of darkness and dread. We must take on what we can of each other's violence and woundedness without allowing ourselves the relief of retaliation. Only if we are prepared to do this do we enter the privilege of the Gospel, which is to heal each other and find our healing in and through each other.

Angela Tilby

You cannot command or compel people into holiness, you cannot increase their spiritual stature one cubit by any kind of force or compulsion. You can do it only by sharing your life with them, by making them feel your goodness, by your love and sacrifice for them.

Rufus M. Jones

*Ye that do your Master's will,*
*Meek in heart be meeker still:*
*Day by day your sins confess,*
*Ye that walk in righteousness:*
*Gracious souls in grace abound,*
*Seek the Lord, whom ye have found.*

*He that comforts all who mourn*
*Shall to joy your sorrow turn:*
*Joy to know your sins forgiven,*
*Joy to keep the way to heaven,*
*Joy to win his welcome grace,*
*Joy to see him face to face.*

*Charles Wesley*

God of all peace and consolation, grant us the gift of your Spirit to enlighten, refresh, enable and sanctify our souls: to be over and around us as the light and dew of heaven, and to fit us for whatever work you are calling us to do; through Jesus Christ our Lord.

Source unknown

If there us any peace and joy in doing any action according to the will of God, he that brings the most of his actions to this rule does most of all to increase the peace and joy of his life.

William Law

To give life
is to be full of sacred wonder and reverence
in front of the mystery of the person;
it is to see the beauty
within and beyond all that is broken.

To love is not to give of your riches
but to reveal to others their riches, their gifts, their value,
and to trust them and their capacity to grow.

So it is important to approach people
in their brokenness and their littleness
gently,
so gently,
not forcing yourself upon them,
but accepting them as they are,
with humility and respect.

> Jean Vanier

Goodness is love in action, love with its hand to the
plough, love with the burden on its back, love following
his footsteps who went about continually doing good.

> J. Hamilton

*There is no love which does not become
help.*

> *Paul Tillich*

# Fruits of the Spirit at Faslane

# Jan Sutch Pickard

The fruit of the spirit is love, joy peace, patience, kindness, generosity, faithfulness, gentleness and self-control. There is no law against such things . . .

Galatians 5:22-23

I started to think about this passage while picking blackberries in Iona. Only a few yards from the Centre for which I am responsible there is a deep drainage ditch. I walked past it a hundred times, and then noticed a spray of berries just out of reach beyond the barbed wire fence. I found a way into the cutting, past an old bedstead put there to keep the sheep from straying, and discovered sweetness and bounty cascading down the steep grassy banks, hanging inches above the water of the little burn: glossy black and purple berries, ripened by a long hot summer. I called others, and we brought pans and pots and picked and picked, feet in the water, heads among the seeding grasses, the sun blessing us where we worked and laughed. Good fruit, tasted and shared, treasured and made into jam to spread on bread and share at tables.

The problem is that I can write with great ease about picking blackberries. And use that as a way of describing a kind of human experience which brings us together and closer to God. But these abstract words . . . 'Love, joy, peace . . .'

I went on thinking, turning this passage from Galatians over and over in my mind until, several months later, the article was due. I had nothing to say. There was no argument. Love, joy, peace . . . How could anyone dispute their value? We must be *for* them, like motherhood and apple pie – or blackberry and apple! There is certainly no law *against* such things.

But it was in confrontation with the law that I really tasted the fruits of the Spirit.

I am a Member of the Iona Community, and as such am committed to action for justice and peace. Over the years this has included joining vigils against apartheid, marching with CND, forming a human chain for Jubilee 2000, signing petitions, writing letters, singing, praying. I have always kept on the right side of the law. But in February 2001, I joined a Ploughshares group, protesting at the gates of Faslane, the huge dockyard dominating the Gareloch, a beautiful part of Scotland, where the Trident nuclear submarines are based.

These are weapons of mass destruction. Their potential for destroying human life is terrifying. Each Trident submarine carries up to sixteen missiles; each missile carries warheads equivalent to twenty-five Hiroshima bombs. They are in place because there is a theory that peace can be kept by a balance of terror. Their presence is protected by the laws of this land. But in 2000 a Scottish court ruled (in the case of two protesters charged with criminal damage on a site connected with Trident) that the existence of these weapons is a crime against international law. Although as I write that ruling is under appeal, it is clear that a strong legal argument can be made against the presence of Trident in Scotland and the purposes of the base at Faslane. Many people also see a moral argument against war in any form. Even those who say that a 'just war' is possible must question the readiness to use such powerful weapons which would inevitably destroy thousands of innocent lives. Can we then argue that these nuclear submarines, which cost us £1,400,000 every day, are never intended to be used? That is an obscene waste of money which could be used for the welfare of people in these islands, or elsewhere in the world. Is there a law against such things? Surely there should be.

So where do love, joy, peace, patience, kindness, generosity, faithfulness, gentleness and self-control come in? I saw them all at the gates of Faslane, and afterwards in Clydebank police station.

Over the years there have been many small demonstrations against Trident, by committed and persistent people. This time an appeal went out to the churches, and to the clergy in particular, to be visibly present at a blockade of the base on 12th February. I was one of the hundreds of people, from all over Scotland and beyond, who responded. We arrived in the darkness before dawn, with crowds of other protesters and police. Gathered under the banner of the Iona Community (many of whose Members were there), we held the first of three services. I was asked to read the Gospel: Matthew 5: 1-12. As I read the words aloud, I saw around me those people of whom Jesus spoke – people who felt very small and helpless against weapons of war, and yet who were hungering and thirsting for what they believed to be justice; people with commitment and a sense of purpose; people called to be peacemakers – whose way of working for peace put them on the front line. I felt that we were anxious, unsure of what would happen before the end of the day, but I was also convinced that it was right for us to be there. I saw joy and peace and patience on my companions' faces, as the sky lightened over the barbed wire.

I saw the police, surrounding the main gate of the base, and beginning to remove protesters who sat in the road. They too were ordinary men and women, with a job to do, whatever opinion they held about Trident – or about people in dog-collars who sat down in the road. The police were not inhuman. In the main they exercised patience, self-control and courtesy. So did those who were breaking the law by stopping the traffic. There was a good spirit, because we live in a country where people do have a right to say what they believe, and to show what they believe – and even law-breakers have rights. But if you 'breach the peace', you will be arrested. And for many of us there, this was a first experience of breaking the law.

It was in this context, of fear and uncertainty, of crowds and the threat of confrontation, that we celebrated Communion. That service was very real to all of us. This is what Jesus did on the night before he was arrested. This was the meal his disciples shared, afraid of what would happen next, and how they would cope. The broken bread was a reminder of our broken lives and broken world – wounded by weapons of mass destruction, crowned with barbed wire – but also of a God who came to share our lives and then let himself be broken on our behalf.

The words of institution rang in my mind mingled with the Beatitudes which I had read earlier: 'Blessed are those who are persecuted in the cause of right, the kingdom of heaven is theirs.' We were not being persecuted, but we were in a small way putting ourselves on the line – because of what we believed.

I was not there for the third service: an ecumenical liturgy which was attended supportively by several church leaders. By then I had been arrested for 'breach of the peace' – for sitting down in the road, at the gates of Faslane, to protest against weapons which threaten to breach the peace of the whole world. I was photographed and fingerprinted and became (before being proved guilty) a person deprived of the freedom most of us take for granted. I found that powerlessness very hard to cope with. But I was not badly treated: I was, for instance, allowed to take my Bible into the cell. During the hours when we were in custody, when not talking to each other, or singing, I discovered how many stories there are in the New Testament about people in prison, letters from prison, messages of hope about release for the captives. Not abstractions – the real thing.

I realise that for us (the thirty or more clergy and members of the whole people of God who were arrested that day) being the church is about a way of life that expresses what it means to be children of God. Paul sums it up in his letter to the Galatians by qualities called 'the fruits of the spirit'. But these are not abstract, nor impossible perfection. They are very down to earth. They are the blessings of the poor in spirit and the peacemakers.

They are the love that supports our sisters and brothers, and is prepared for sacrificial action; joy in the singing of South African freedom songs in police vans and cells; self-control when doing a difficult job; simple acts of kindness (the Bible in the cell); gentleness in the face of our mutual fear; faithfulness when uncertain what will happen next; generosity of spirit; gentleness in the face of anger; peace in the face of war. There is no law against such things.

Help us accept each other
As Christ accepted us;
Teach us as sister, brother,
Each person to embrace.
Be present, Lord, among us
And bring us to believe:
We are *ourselves* accepted
And meant to love and live.

Teach us, O Lord, your lessons,
As in our daily life
We struggle to be human
And search for hope and faith.
Teach us to care for people,
For all – not just for some,
To love them as we find them
Or as they may become.

Let your acceptance change us
So that we may be moved
In living situations
To do the truth in love;
To practice your acceptance
Until we know by heart
The table of forgiveness
And laughter's healing art.

Lord, for today's encounters
With all who are in need,
Who hunger for acceptance,
For righteousness and bread,
We need new eyes for seeing,
New hands for holding on:
Renew us with your Spirit;
Lord, free us, make us one!

Fred Kaan

*If you do not wish for his kingdom, don't pray for it. But if you do, you must work for it . . . It is not to be a kingdom of the dead, but of the living.*

*John Ruskin*

Whatever more than others you have received in health, natural gifts, working capacity, success, a beautiful childhood, harmonious family circumstances, you must not accept as being a matter of course. You must pay a price for them. You must show more than average devotion of life to life.

Albert Schweitzer

Love is not only something you feel. It's something you do.

David Wilkerson

To love anyone is nothing else than to wish that person good.

St. Thomas Aquinas

*Fruits of the Spirit*

Reach out my hand to touch
My neighbour, friend,
Or kith and kin.

Not quite;
Not far enough;
The gap's too great.
So I must lean
Further and further,
Hand stretching out to hand.

What if I fall;
Lose balance and
    Upset
My equilibrium?

Perhaps I shall have to change my ground . . .

But do I stand on holy ground?

Donald Hilton

The energy of Love discharges itself along the lines which
form a triangle whose points are God, self, and neighbour.

C. F. Dodd

*To give one's life, on weary days and hopeless,*
*To give one's life, hour after hour, and be*
*Ready to give again, again – is harder*
*Than to give in a moment, gloriously.*

*Anonymous*

Permit your friends to be themselves. Accept them as they are. be grateful for what is there, not annoyed by what friends cannot give. Accept each one's imperfections and individuality, and don't feel threatened if their opinions and tastes differ from yours.

Give praise and encouragement. Tell your friends what you like about them, how thankful you are for their presence in your life. Delight in their talents, applaud their successes.

Source unknown

Good Shepherd of men's souls, give to us patience and understanding that we may seek the lost; and endue us with thy grace of shepherding that we may lead them gently home. Amen.

Anonymous

Blessed is he that does good to others and desires not that others should do good to him.

Brother Giles

*Spiritually it makes little difference what our work is; it is the manner of our doing it.*

*Hugh Black*

The basic Christian faith is in the God in whom Christ profoundly and constantly believed, a faith for which he was prepared to die. It is only at rare moments that most of us ever attain a faith of real quality. These may be moments in which we have fleetingly entered into the suffering of others, or when we have been comforted by a hope that we may have been forgiven for some deficiency or selfishness.

Roy Niblett

All growth is trouble.
If comfort is your need,
Better to sleep
Curled round yourself for ever,
Shelled with indifference,
Like an unknown seed.

All love is trouble.
Once you give your heart
To anything, to anyone at all,
You are made vulnerable
In every part.

To be at peace in love,
At peace and free,
Is the hope of fools.
If fool you be,
Curl snugly round yourself
Like a smooth stone
Or put forth leaves
Or know
What the great have known.

R. H. Grenville

# Don't Curse the Darkness

# Pat Robson

Over the last two decades the Iron Curtain has risen across Eastern Europe to expose nations of people ill-prepared to perform on an international stage. Nevertheless the public, who had waited in anticipation for so long, demanded that the show should start, and the more uncomfortable the players seemed by their sudden exposure, the more insistent the audience became and the more they demanded to see.

And what did they see?

They saw once proud nations that had been stamped into submission by the jackboots of corrupt regimes. They saw peoples who had lived in fear for so long that they were unable to comprehend the freedom that had suddenly become theirs. They saw men and women, conditioned by years of obedience, bewildered by the very suddenness of it all, anxiously looking about them for someone to tell them how to behave, how to speak, how to think. They saw human beings who, in order to survive in an arena of fear, had put aside loyalty and truth, kindness and generosity, affection and joy. Every word spoken was suspicious, every thought potentially seditious. As the curtain lifted it was on to this stage of intrigue and fear that the eyes of the world were turned, and the evil and the darkness were dramatically exposed.

All over the world there are people living in fear. Wherever a person or a government uses the force of power to keep others in submission then there is evil and darkness and misery. It doesn't matter if it is one man who is ill-treating his wife or whether it is a tyrant, dictator government that is suppressing the freedom of a nation, a single person who suffers is as important as a hundred, a thousand single people who suffer. The darkness is there, the evil is there.

I have lived in Africa and felt the darkness of the fear that lies just below the surface in everybody's life: the fear that talks of escape routes, apartheid, guns and machetes. The fear that is fed by suspicion, poverty, resentment and hatred.

I have worked in Eastern Europe and have wept to see potentially caring doctors too afraid to unlock storeroom doors and allow warm clothing to be distributed among shivering mental patients. I have felt the horror of seeing helpless children die of neglect because they have been deemed incapable of contributing anything of value to society. I have been bewildered and frustrated by officials the world over who will do nothing to relieve the suffering of others while they are in a position to do so and yet, when they are in the bosom of their family, display all the love and generosity you could wish for.

The power of evil in this world is insidious. Spawned in darkness and fed by fear it coils itself around its victims until they are crushed by despair.

From the comfort of our armchairs these words seem overly dramatic for, in our world of quiet sophistication and reasoned passions, we have become used to 'turning off' the news if it offends the ear. We hastily close doors and build walls to protect ourselves from pain. We push back the darkness and surround ourselves with a cushion of grey, unthreatening comfort. We forget that those who don't experience the blackness of night can never truly know the joy of dawn. We dull our senses so that even the most momentous event in the history of man, the event that pierced the darkness of the world with a shattering brilliance of joy, has become nothing more to us than a much loved story between the pages of a book.

Is that truly so? Does it mean so little to us or do we perhaps find it too mind-boggling to comprehend? Can we really believe that the very Spirit of God that hovered over the surface of the world at its creation came into the world and went about on earth, and, as Jesus of Nazareth, lived and breathed and dwelt among us? And if that wasn't miracle enough we read, in the Acts of the Apostles, that after the death of Jesus, when the disciples were gathered together, afraid and in hiding, there came a strong and driving wind which filled them with the burning intensity of fire. And as we read we realise with growing amazement that the death of Jesus was not the end; that the Spirit of the almighty God was once more loose on the earth, living and breathing and moving in those he had left behind. The one light had become a multitude of flames, each set to banish the darkness of evil.

The early Christians were desperately aware of the enormity of their task. It was dangerous being a Christian. The light they carried could so easily be snuffed out. But, dangerous or not, what is so totally amazing is that two thousand years later the flames of their faith are still burning, handed down from generation to generation. Ever since that first day of Pentecost the fire of the Holy Spirit has never been quenched. More and more people come forward to be baptised. A never-ending stream of people receive the gift of the Holy Spirit and are prepared to face evil and even death itself in order to take the light of Christ to others.

It's eleven years now since I first travelled to Eastern Europe and things are changing. People are discovering that the faith of their grandparents is not the opium of the masses as they were led to believe, but something vibrant and life-giving, something that restores their sense of self-worth, filling them with joy and allowing them to love and be loved once more.

How wonderful it is to see a mother, conditioned all her life to believe that handicapped children are a blight on society, pick up a paralysed child and hold it to her breast, crooning and rocking and loving the child to sleep. How heartening it is to see the young Westerner with the punk hair-do, the nose ring and the tattoos, take a child whose legs are thin and wasted from years of being tied in a foul-smelling cot, and patiently teach him to walk and to laugh and to live again. What a miracle it is to see people, who have lived a lifetime under a harsh Communist regime, walk for miles to a small village church to give thanks to God for all of this life's goodness.

And in Africa? The white missionaries of my era, who were so brutally hacked to death, have been replaced by their pupils. Young black pastors, on fire with the Spirit of God, are lighting fires that are raging against all odds, and now black missionaries are being sent to the UK to help us to rekindle the flickering flames of our faltering faith.

Never doubt it. The Spirit of God is at loose in the world and the harvest of the Spirit is ripening. Love, joy, peace, patience, kindness, goodness, fidelity, gentleness and self-control, all are flowering in the warmth and light of lives freed from the darkness of evil.

Change is all about us. In my lifetime the Berlin Wall has fallen, the Iron Curtain has been lifted. Apartheid has been abandoned and peace talks are taking place in Northern Ireland. Don't switch off the news. Don't close your eyes, your ears, your hearts to the despair of others. Look instead beyond the horror and see those whom God has touched working quietly in the ruin of people's lives to heal the wounds. See the doctors, the nurses, the pastors, the teachers, the aid workers, the politicians and the ordinary men and women who are reaching out with love.

Pray and go, or pray and give, but don't curse the darkness and do nothing. Light a candle and be part of the flame.

*I have known sorrow, therefore I*
*may laugh with you, O friend,*
*more merrily*
*than those who never sorrowed*
*upon earth,*
*and knew what laughter's worth.*

*I have known laughter, therefore I*
*may sorrow with you far more*
*tenderly*
*than those who never knew how sad a thing*
*seems merriment to one's*
*heart-suffering.*

*Elizabeth Barrett Browning*

O God, you put into my heart this great desire to devote myself to the sick and sorrowful. I offer it to you. Do with it what is for thy service.

Florence Nightingale

Love sees not only what it could do if conditions were favourable, but also what it can do under conditions as they are.

T. E. Jessop

Here is a picture of our opportunity. It is as though God offered us a partnership, giving us a garden. We must till it. There is dignity in our labour because there is life in seed and sun and soil. If we work, then the gift of God will come in fruit and flower. If we laze, what was a garden will become a wilderness.

Source unknown

In my daughter's garden there is a pear tree whose topmost branch was broken during a winter storm and hung almost vertical from the tree. It was too high to reach, so it was left to die and fall off. However, in spring it budded and blossomed and in the autumn bore a few small pears. It was obviously still part of the tree, though its hold was rather precarious. For two seasons since then it has borne larger fruit and as it grows it is increasing its hold on the tree, and the life-sap reaches it more effectively each year. Which story is to me a parable of the life in the Spirit.

Ida Church

Seed time and harvest are separated in time, but inseparable in fact. Our Lord sowed without reaping, but the ages will reap the harvest. Spiritual work is done for eternity. Be patient in your husbandry.

Source unknown

All through this day, O Lord, let me touch as many lives as possible for thee. And every life I touch by thy Holy Spirit quicken, whether through the word I speak, the prayer I breathe or the life I live.

Catherine Greenshields

*Dismiss me not thy service, Lord,*
*But train me for thy will;*
*And I will ask for no reward*
*Except to serve thee still.*

*T. T. Lynch*

It is within my power either to serve God or not to serve him. Serving him I add to my own good and the good of the whole world. Not serving him I forfeit my own good and deprive the world of that good, which was in my power to create.

Leo Tolstoy

*If thou love each thing thou wilt perceive the mystery of God in all; and when once thou perceive this, thou wilt thenceforward grow every day to a fuller understanding of it; until thou come at last to love the whole world with a love that will then be all-embracing and universal.*

*Love will teach us all things: but we must learn how to win love; it is got with difficulty: it is a possession dearly bought with much labour and in a long time; for one must love not sometimes only, for a passing moment, but always.*

*Feodor Dostoevsky*

O God, uphold us by the consciousness that our work is useful work and a blessing to all . . . May there be nothing in this day's work of which we shall be ashamed when the sun has set, nor in the eventide of our life when our task is done.

Walter Rauschenbusch

Through the gift of the Holy Spirit we become witnesses on his behalf. To us he has entrusted the message of hope, the task of bringing light to them that sit in darkness . . . The world's redemption, the saving of human beings, is something God does for us. It is the gift of God. But we have our part to play. We, too, are people sent from God.

Allen Birtwhistle

*In his will is our peace.*

*Dante Alighieri*

*O Lord, renew our spirits and draw our hearts to you, that our work may not be to us a burden, but a delight, and give us such a mighty love to you as may sweeten all our obedience.*

*Benjamin Jenks*

Teach me, good Lord,
Not to murmur at multitude of business or shortness of
    time.
Not to magnify undertaken duties by seeming to suffer
under them, but to treat all as liberties and gladnesses.
Not to call attention to crowded work, or pretty fatigues.
Not to gather encouragement from appreciation by others,
Lest this should interfere with purity of motive.
Not to seek praise, respect, gratitude, or regard from
superiors or equals on account of age or past service.
Not to let myself be placed in favourable contrast with
another.

Edward White Benson

*Forgive us, Lord, that we have remembered things we have done for others and forgotten what they have done for us. Help us to cease complaining and, knowing thy presence with us, may we begin to serve with good cheer.*

*Anonymous*

# Keeping it Real

## Anthony Reddie

One of the most rewarding aspects of the area in which I work (The Queen's Foundation for Ecumenical Theological Education and the Methodist Church), is the opportunity it provides for me to meet a great many people, in a variety of situations. The young people are among the most challenging of those I meet. They often show a healthy cynicism for so-called 'important people' since they are young enough to be unimpressed by individuals often deemed to be their betters. I have found a good number of Black young people who have an attitude that seems to say, 'Impress me, then! Show me why you're considered so important, that I should listen to you?'

In truth, I have yet to meet a young person who has ever said that to me, but I often have a perception of these feelings when looking into the eyes of such individuals. When I was thinking about the 'fruits of the Spirit' as detailed in Galatians 5:22-26, it struck me that many of the qualities listed in this passage speak of a concern to be *genuine* and to have *integrity* in our dealings with others, qualities which young people especially value. Let me say a little more about this.

In the last six years or so, my life has changed enormously. The speed and the nature of that change continually surprises me. When I embarked upon a seemingly innocuous research project a number of years ago, as a Christian Education Worker, Donald Eadie, a dear friend of mine, said to me that this was 'an extraordinary opportunity I had been given'. As a wise and deeply spiritual man, I guess that Donald knew what he was talking about, but the extent of that opportunity has only just begun to sink in.

Moving from being an anonymous youth and community worker to become a recognised writer and educationist is an enormous change. Having people request your services to preach, teach or write is a tremendous boost for one's ego. And yet, within the process of this change, I often find myself feeling profoundly uneasy. I have seen people's attitude to me change. The recognition one receives is tinged with elements of discomfort, as some people are apt to offer disproportionate amounts of praise that is usually undeserved.

When this process is repeated over an extended period of time, the dangers of losing one's self to the continuing perils of arrogance, smugness and self-importance are very real concerns that any individual ignores at their peril.

Leslie Griffiths, another wise (I shall refrain from using the word 'old') sage, to whom I have had cause to be extremely grateful, once advised me that I should get myself a good group of friends and colleagues, who could ensure that I remained 'grounded'. Such individuals would see to it that I did not lose myself to the continual trickle of flattery that would inevitably come my way. Once again, I have had cause to thank a trusted colleague for his good advice.

In the last few years, I have, through the wise counsel of such friends, attempted to remain grounded. As I consider the many fruits of the spirit, such as patience, kindness and goodness, I am reminded of the continual challenge to gain and retain a sense of genuineness and integrity in my dealings with others, particularly with those who are closest to me and know me best. My attempts to 'live by the Spirit' and 'keep in touch with the Spirit' have been made, both by what I have tried to develop within my own life and practice, but, more importantly, through what the

Holy Spirit has done for me through the kind mediation of others.

In terms of my own practice, I have tried (with varying degrees of success) to find time to be still, in order to listen to the silence, in which the whispers of the spirit can be discerned. I am not a great one for retreats. I know this aspect of the Christian life is important for many people. For me, however, going on retreat is somewhat akin to my attempts to write poetry (at which I am hopeless), in that I am so self-conscious in trying to be 'spiritual' and 'reflective' that the whole exercise becomes painfully arched and utterly pretentious.

Instead of going on retreat, I often find myself parking my car in many parts of Birmingham, usually in places where the daily bustle of inner city life is clearly evident. In such places, I lean back in the seat and simply let my mind drift, in the silence (comparatively speaking, given the noise and bustle of the world around me) of the moment. Sometimes, alarmingly 'big ideas' come rushing into my mind, only to promptly disappear, unless I take out my pen to do my habitual scribbling.

On one such occasion, when I was parked, dreaming my life away, a police officer came by on a motorcycle and tapped on my side window. He wanted to know if I was all right. I sensed in his voice a concern that I was on the verge of taking my own life. On the contrary, I was giving my life back to God.

I hope that I am not presenting myself as a deeply pious and particularly spiritual person. Those who know me well would laugh out loud at such an assessment. And yet, despite my life-long cynicism towards many things 'spiritual', I am deeply conscious of the way in which my life has progressed in recent times. The change is not, I believe, to be understood solely in terms of the hard work and the study I have undertaken in that time. I have been aware of the prompting of the Spirit continually reflecting not only upon my work, but also on my dealings with others. The latter is more important than the former. On a number of occasions I have felt compelled to look again at a given situation, and to reconsider a particular course of action. These moments often bring about acute, temporary moments of clarity, and sharpness of vision. At such moments, no matter how transitory, the fruits of the spirit have been clearly discerned.

On a number of occasions, however, my semi-nomadic wanderings in my car have not yielded any great epiphanies. The development of the fruits of the spirit within my life has come through others. When writing about experiences and thoughts, I rarely mention people by name, but I have broken all my unofficial rules in this piece. In addition to Donald Eadie and Leslie Griffiths, I want to name Tony Malcolm, Charles Severs and Carol Troupe. One of Tony's great dictums (I'm not sure if he first coined it, but I have heard him say it on a number of occasions), is 'If people say bad things about you, live your life in such a way as to prove them wrong.' I would never claim to be a saint, but I have taken those words to heart, and Tony's friendship has been one of my great inspirations.

From Charles Severs, I have gained a grudging respect for the merits of retreats and periods of pre-planned silence despite the doubts I mentioned earlier. He once insisted that I go with him to a small retreat house near Chepstow, which is run by Roman Catholic nuns. To say that I was sceptical would be a gross understatement. But those twenty-four hours were a gift from God. The peace of mind and the clear perspective that emerged restored my diminished sanity. Charles prays for me every Wednesday at 7am. Through this great friendship, I have learnt the art of gentleness and self-control. On one memorable occasion a horrendous accusation was levelled at him by someone who had formerly been a close friend. My natural response would have been combative and strident, but he asked, instead, that we pray for that person. He felt that only someone in deep pain could have said those things, and as such, they needed the gift of healing, which only God could provide. I was staggered.

Finally there is Carol Troupe. A deeply private person, about whom I will say very little, for she will curse me at length if I say too much – which is anything at all. About Carol I will simply say this. She is the least pretentious person I have ever met. If I want to hear the 'real deal' without any hint of flattery or frills, then Carol is guaranteed to 'tell me as it is'. In her honesty and friendship Carol represents the gift of faithfulness.

For her, as for all the people whom I would consider to be my friends, I am eternally grateful. Your presence is invaluable. Thank you!

*In all our attitudes,*
*keep us humble, courageous and enterprising;*
*ready to face anger and persecution;*
*prepared for disappointment and frustration;*
*living always as those*
*who already possess your peace,*
*and by our delight in it*
*making it real for the world.*

*Alan Gaunt*

This kind of love sometimes becomes manifest when there is a conflict between the demands of heavenly and earthly love. 'Here I am, Lord, send me to the ends of the earth; send me from all that is called comfort in earth; send me even to death itself if it be but in thy service and in thy kingdom.

Henry Martyn

*It is in the effects and deeds following afterward that one discerns the value of prayer . . . If we fail to love our neighbour, we are lost.*

*Teresa of Avila*

Loving means to love the unlovable, or it is no virtue at all.

G. K. Chesterton

Grant to us, O Lord, the Invincible Spirit:
that we might always be victorious in our fight with the
evil forces of the world.
Grant to us, O Lord, the Adventurous Spirit:
that we may not be afraid to tread a path that is strange to
us.
Grant to us, O Lord, the Courageous Spirit:
that we may dare anything to serve and follow thee
sincerely.
Grant to us, O Lord, the Spirit of Endurance:
that we may not grow weary in our efforts to do right.
Grant to us, O Lord, the Hopeful Spirit:
that we may never despair even when things go wrong,
and life seems hard and difficult.
Grant to us, O Lord, the Cheerful Spirit:
that we may show all people there is joy in obeying thy
will.
Grant to us, O Lord, the Spirit of Gratitude:
that we may acknowledge thee as our Loving Protector
and Father, the Source of all good.

Vera Pewtress

Sow good seed at every opportunity, relying on the
sequences of God. Sow in faith. When you cast your seed
on the earth, cast yourself on the love and faithfulness of
God – whether the seed be wheat, a good deed or a kindly
thought. With you rests the responsibility of sowing, with
God the responsibility of harvest.

Leslie Church

*I will tell you the secret. God has had all there was of me. There have been men with greater brains than I, men with greater opportunities; but from the day I got the poor of London on my heart, and a vision of what Christ could do with the poor of London, I made up my mind that God would have all of William Booth there was. And if there is anything of power in the Salvation Army today, it is because God has all the adoration of my heart and all the power of my will, and all the influence of my life.*

*William Booth*

One of the most surprising marks of our Lord's words is their *gentleness*. He never exaggerates, never wishes to make people out worse than they are. He tries to think the best of people, and when he must point out their faults to warn them, he does it with a gentleness that no one could deny, or say that he has spoken too hardly, or not shown that gentleness is the absolute truth.

Edward King

Goodness is something so simple: always to live for others, never to seek one's own advantage.

Dag Hammarskjöld

Let love and appreciation have their way. So many tired hearts might go on their way singing at the mere price of a handclasp, a whisper of encouragement, or a look which told that loving service has not passed unnoticed.

Anonymous

*What God has put in our power is the happiness of those about us, and that is largely to be secured by being kind to them.*

*Anonymous*

Keep me from turning back!
My hand is on the plough, my faltering hand:
But all in front of me is untilled land,
Keep me from turning back.

Source unknown

Love transfigures life's landscapes with new and brighter colours. It transforms life's labour into joyful privilege.

T. Howard Crago

*I thank thee for the beauty, O Most High,*
*Of this Cathedral built with love and art,*
*Which I would see, not with the vacant eye*
*Of wonder, but with sympathetic heart,*
*Loving the beauty of this House of Prayer.*
*I pray thee for all those who serve thee here,*
*That they may hold thy Glory their first care;*
*And for all those who come from far and near*
*Thy blessing I would crave; and for all men*
*who love this place I pray. Then for the sad*
*And lonely, that thy mercy may abound,*
*And for the happy folk, thy grace. And then*
*I ask this for myself. Let me go, glad,*
*Refreshed, uplifted, to my daily round.*

*A Prayer for Sightseers, Exeter Cathedral*

Lord, you have the clear, sparkling water of life within you; and you share humanity's experience of shed blood; we pray for all who suffer, that they may know your solidarity in the intensity of their pain, and also receive the advocacy of the Holy Spirit to comfort and uplift them. Help them to find a faith that protects their inmost self from destruction; to experience the love and peace of God which no suffering can shut out if our faith keeps us open to you: to find an assurance of spiritual life which is renewed in vigour each day. We also pray that in our human mortality they may find hope of salvation as it is received in bread, healing, companionship, rest for body and mind, affirmation for the person they are, real achievement and meaningful goals, and joy, fresh each morning. And for those who will not find relief in this life we pray that you will impart courage and faith that their life was not lived in vain. Through Jesus Christ our Lord.

Denis Vernon

# The Spirit at Work

# E. Philip Schofield

My sister was sixteen years older than I and at the age of eighteen she left home to train as a nurse. I looked forward eagerly to her day off when she came home and, like the wise men of old, she came bearing gifts! As my sixth birthday approached I dropped more than one hint that I would like a train-set and, seeing her coming up the road, I ran to greet her.

She carried no parcel in her hand, and there was nothing more than a big hug as she wished me a happy birthday. Ah well, I thought, she'll have hidden it at home. Not so. There was no train-set. With a kiss she said, 'Happy Birthday!' and gave me a small parcel. I opened it, puzzled and disappointed, and discovered to my bitter anguish that it was a Bible.

Furious at what I thought a despicable gift, I flung it on the floor and it skidded under a chest of drawers. My sister broke down in tears as she bent to retrieve it, but Mother said, 'No, lass, he threw it down – let him pick it up!' I pass over the immediate distress to the day, a week or so later, when I did pick up the Bible, its outer cover torn off, and put it on a shelf to be forgotten.

It was not forgotten, and it was to become one of my most treasured possessions. At school I became fascinated with many of the Bible stories, mainly because of my English master. He would have us read, and sometimes learn, whole passages. Frequently he would stop us and say, 'No! Put some feeling into your words. This is the most beautiful English ever written – treat it as such!' And he

174

himself would read the passages which wonderfully came alive.

Years later I was accepted for training to become a minister and, on vacation from university I visited my old school particularly to say thank you to my old English master. I was in for a surprise. He listened to me in the courteous way I would have expected and then asked, 'Did I ever teach you about the Christian faith? Did I ever tell you to believe in God?' I had to admit that he hadn't. 'Because,' he said, 'I am an atheist – I taught you only the beauty of the English language.'

We talked about the mystery of faith, and my sense of call to the ministry, and I found him to be as thought-provoking and stimulating as ever. He had to go off for a class, so we agreed to meet up again the following week. Sadly we did not meet. I turned up at the school to learn that he had died suddenly the day before. Walking slowly away I pondered the mystery of life and death, and of how God – working through an atheist – had given me so much inspiration. He does indeed work in mysterious ways.

Back to my sister. She was now nursing in Liverpool and told me of an experience she had when walking by the docks. A crowd attracted her attention and she went along to hear a soap-box orator, gifted in holding the attention of his listeners, and proclaiming for all to hear that he was an atheist, that the church was rubbish, that parsons were parasites – and worse. Then he threw down a challenge: 'If there's anyone here prepared to speak up for Jesus – come on and do it now!' For a while there was silence, then slowly two young girls pushed their way to the front and, standing before the crowd, one of them said, 'We're not much good at speaking up for Jesus, but we'll sing for him.' Together, timidly at first but with growing strength they sang, 'Stand up, stand up for Jesus'. The crowd was silent and, when the girls had finished singing, most of them drifted away, obviously moved by what they had heard.

My studies took me into the intricacies of theology, the delicate questions of faith, the traditional beliefs of the church down through the years, the changes in attitude and in ecclesiology whereby different understandings created different branches of what I believed – and still believe – is one church. I knew I must understand my faith, and the reasons for it, if I were to minister to whatever congregation I was called upon to serve. Perhaps more important, I had to be able to speak in ways that could be understood by those unfamiliar with the language of the church.

An understanding of the nature of God was essential. Father, Son and Holy Spirit – but what did this mean, and how might it be presented in terms which clearly defined that which is at the heart of the Christian faith? In what way did they, the Trinity, relate one to the other? Father Creator, yes. Christ the Son, yes. But Holy Spirit? A rushing mighty wind? Tongues of fire? The *pneuma kuriou* of the New Testament was a literal translation of *ruach adonai* in the Old Testament – the Spirit, or more literally, the wind of the Lord. I wanted to know more.

At the heart of my ministry was to be God in Christ, through the Holy Spirit, within the church, and I was attracted by the emphasis which Schleimacher made on being not so much a study of the science of God as of the science of the church's *experience* of God. He concerned himself not so much with the Deity of the Holy Spirit as with the Spirit's function within the Christian community. To me that was real. It focused on the reality and consequences of Christian experience. I also saw the church not as a fellowship confined within four walls, but as breaking out – under the power of the Holy Spirit – into the community as a whole, embracing in a remarkable way folk of different beliefs through whose sincerity the Holy Spirit might work.

I cannot but believe that the Spirit was at work in my sister's gift of a Bible, in my atheistic English teacher, and in the two young girls who witnessed so wonderfully on the dockside in Liverpool.

So what of the church?

St. Paul recognised and acknowledged that within the fellowship of Christ's people there would be different gifts, specific abilities, each one of which could and should complement the others. The church is the Body of Christ, 'a single body which has many parts', and no one part can say to another, 'I don't need you.' In recognising the gifts of the Holy Spirit he acknowledged that some were of greater importance, greater significance, than others. The enthusiasm of the so-called charismatic is to be welcomed, but more to be desired are love, joy, peace, long-suffering, gentleness, goodness, faith, meekness, temperance, against which there is no law. These, says Paul in Galatians, are the fruit of the Spirit, and he exhorts his readers so to live that the Spirit might be seen in, and experienced through, their lives and their fellowship.

It is against the background of this approach to an understanding of the Holy Spirit, Schleimacher's theology of the Spirit at work in, and identified with, the church, that we are able to understand Irenaeus' concept of 'the two hands of God', by which he saw God's hands at work in Christ and in his church. For this reason it is rightly said that the church is the body of Christ, and we who profess to be Christian, part of that body, ought to walk in the Spirit, showing forth in our lives the fruit of the Spirit and expressing it in a loving, caring relationship one with another. We should not be, as Paul puts it, 'desirous of vain glory, provoking one another, envying one another' (Galatians 5:26).

My heart aches. I began my ministry more than fifty years ago, glorying in the concept of one church which, despite its different traditions, could yet be united in its common concern to represent, and to be, the one body of Christ. It saddens me that, despite the setting up of commissions and the existence of a World Council of Churches, we cannot yet share fully in the Sacrament, and divisions still exist which separate one communion from another. How can we claim to live in the Spirit, to walk in the Spirit, when so often in our human frailty we lay stress upon traditional beliefs which, understandable as they are, dismember the body of Christ?

I end on a lighter note. Some time ago an old lady told me that she had been on holiday and wanted to attend church, 'but not,' she said, 'one of those hand-clapping, foot-stamping services'. During the week prior to the Sunday, she saw a gardener mowing the church lawn and asked him, 'Is it charismatic?' to which the gardener replied, looking down at his mower, 'No, it's petrol driven!' Perhaps Paul should have added one more fruit to the gifts of the Spirit – that of a sense of humour! Rightly used it can break many a barrier down.

Blessed Lord, I beseech you to send your grace upon me, such as may not only cleanse this life of mine, but beautify it a little. Grant that I may love you with all my heart and soul and mind and strength, and love my neighbour as myself – and that I may persevere to the end, through the loving kindness of God, in Jesus Christ.

James Skinner

*Give strength, give thought, give deeds, give wealth,*
*Give love, give tears, and give thyself.*
*Give, give, be always giving;*
*Who gives not is not living:*
*The more you give, the more you live.*

*Anonymous*

A Christian should always remember that the value of his good works is not based on their number and excellence, but on the love of God which prompts him to do these things.

Juan de la Cruz

O God, I give thee humble and hearty thanks for thy great goodness toward me . . . Give me patience and courage, a firm resolution to do thy service, with grace to do it.

Archbishop Laud

The church is not meant to be filled with a bunch of self-confident types; it is composed of people who know that without God's help they are no good to man or beast, and it is surprising, when you get to know them from the inside, as I do, how different they look. They may look dull and uninspiring to the outward eye, but sometimes a God's-eye view of them has come my way, and has shown them to be what they really are, a bunch of ordinary human beings which, relying on God, is full of many mini-Mother Teresas and pocket Wesleys and Wilberforces in tired and dilapidated cassocks doing their best to love God and their fellows; and at such times, I wouldn't swop them for any other bunch in God's world.

Anthony Bridge

*The impulse of love that leads us to the doorway of a friend is the voice of God within and we need not be afraid to follow it.*

*Agnes Sanford*

If you haven't learned to love someone else better than yourself, you haven't begun to live.

Catherine Bramwell-Booth

180

Create in us the splendour that dawns when
   hearts are kind,
That knows not race or colour as boundaries of
   the mind;
That learns to value beauty, in heart, or brain,
   or soul,
And longs to bind God's children into one
   perfect whole.

Anonymous

Your actions in passing, pass not away, for every good
work is a grain of seed for eternal life.

Bernard of Clairvaux

It is possible to give without loving, but it is impossible to
love without giving.

Richard Braunstein

*Be tender with the young,*
*Compassionate with the aged,*
*Sympathetic with the striving*
*And tolerant of the weak and strong.*
*Indeed, at some time in our own lives,*
*We could be all of these.*

*George Washington Carver*

Holy Spirit,
in our homes and community
but especially in the household of faith,
*may we walk in love.*


Holy Spirit,
when we worship and witness
and when we share the sufferings of our neighbours,
*may we walk in joy.*


Holy Spirit,
in places of confrontation,
racial unrest, stark inequality and deep-seated violence,
*may we walk in peace.*


Holy Spirit,
in a frantic and fearful world
where there are pressures to gain quick results,
*may we walk in patience.*


Holy Spirit,
as we seek to respect other people's personalities,
their gifts and skills, their jobs and dreams,
*may we walk in kindness.*

Holy Spirit,
in our determination to reject what is unjust,
hypocritical and an affront to the Gospel,
*may we walk in goodness.*


Holy Spirit,
where we have made commitments to those close to us
and promises to love you and our neighbours,
*may we walk in faithfulness.*


Holy Spirit,
when we are tempted to respond with anger
to embittering situations which are already filled with
        pain,
*may we walk in gentleness.*


Holy Spirit,
in our private living and public responsibilities
and in all our decision-making,
*may we walk with self-control.*


Holy Spirit,
fill us and all people with these gifts now and always.


David Jenkins

# Contributors

**Jill Baker,** a few weeks after studying theology at Durham University and marrying a Maths teacher, found herself as a ministerial student's wife at Wesley College, Bristol. Following this a surprise route led to an offer to work for the Overseas Division of the Methodist Church. In January 1994, with Timothy, aged four years, and Peter, just fourteen weeks old, she and her husband Andrew arrived in Chateaubelair, St. Vincent, and after four years there they moved on to Grenada. They are now back in the UK in circuit ministry in the Stoke (South) circuit. Jill is the author of *Here and There: Advent reflections from two cultures* (Methodist Publishing House).

**Rev Roland Bamford** was brought up in the Lancashire cotton town of Oldham. He trained for the Methodist ministry in Manchester and studied Hebrew and cognate languages at the University. He describes his ministry as a pastoral one, ministering Christ through caring, listening, enabling and encouraging people, and leading worship. In 1965 he married Glennys, then a Methodist deaconess and they began a joint ministry while their children, Ruth and Rachel, were growing up. In 1984 Glennys was ordained and she and Roland worked together in Wolverhampton and Luton until they retired in 1997. Roland now helps pastorally in his local Methodist circuit of Wolverhampton (Trinity). He writes the occasional piece for the *Methodist Recorder* and has compiled two joke books for Christian Aid.

**Rev Michael Begg** is a Methodist minister who served for twenty years in churches in East Anglia, Jamaica and Kent, and for nearly fourteen years with Christian Aid in the UK and the Republic of Ireland. With his wife Andrea he now runs retreats for up to six people at Avelin, at Ballymore Eustace, Co. Kildare, which is a member of the Methodist Retreat Group (email: begg@iol.ie). He is an associate minister in a group of six Church of Ireland parishes in Co. Wicklow.

**Major Nigel Bovey** has been a Salvation Army officer since 1979 and is editor of *The War Cry*. He has served as a corps officer, with his wife Margaret, in Lisburn, Londonderry, Teddington, Liverpool and Worcester. In 1994 he was appointed as editorial assistant on *The War Cry*, becoming its deputy editor in 1996 and editor in 1999. Before officership Nigel was a teacher of Mathematics, Economics and Sociology at St. Mark's RC Comprehensive School, Harlow. He is the author of three books, *How To Tell A Children's Story*, *The Mercy Seat* and *Christians In The House* – a collection of interviews with forty-nine Christian MPs. His choral work, *Let Me Fly*, was recorded in 1998. Nigel has one daughter, Janine, and one son, Andrew. He loves playing cricket and walking Dartmoor.

**Rev Elizabeth Canham** grew up in England and was a lecturer in Biblical Studies before moving to the USA in 1981 to be ordained as an Episcopal Priest. She has served parishes in London, New Jersey, New York and North Carolina, and is Founder/Director of a Retreat Ministry in Black Mountain, NC. Dr Canham is author of four books: *Pilgrimage to Priesthood*, *Praying the Bible*, *Journaling with Jeremiah*, and *Heart Whispers* now available in the UK.

**Rt Rev and Rt Hon Richard Chartres** is the one hundred and thirty-second Bishop of London. After service as a curate in Bedford and as Chaplain to the Archbishop of Canterbury he worked as a parish priest in Victoria for nine years. In 1992 he was consecrated as Bishop of Stepney and spent some very happy years in the East End seeing at first hand some of the excellent work that continues to be done by the Methodist Church in some of Britain's poorest boroughs. Richard was appointed Bishop of London in 1995, and one of his most pleasant recent tasks was to install Rev Leslie Griffiths, Minister of Wesley's Chapel, as an Honorary Canon of St. Paul's Cathedral.

**Rev Steve Cullis** is a Methodist minister in the Peterborough circuit, and is married to Julie. He is grateful to Rev Dr David Wilkinson's astronomy 'lessons' while they were both being trained for the ministry – he always felt they might come in handy! He previously served in the Diss circuit of the Methodist Church, in the East Anglia District.

**Rev Dr Denis Duncan** is a minister of The Church of Scotland, former Editor of *British Weekly,* former Director of The Churches' Council of Health and Healing, and former Associate Director and Training Supervisor of Westminster Pastoral Foundation, of Highgate Counselling Centre and of Hampstead Counselling Service, all in London. He was Chairman of The World Association for Pastoral Care and Counselling and of the World Congress of that body in 1979. He has written some two hundred and seventy-five Meditations for the *Daily Telegraph.* Collections of these have been published as *Be Still and Know . . . Solitude, Stillness and Serenity* and *Rainbows Through the Rain.* He is the author and editor of eight other titles. His book, *The Harvest of the Spirit,* is available from 80a Woodland Rise, London N10 3UJ (Fax 020 8374 4008), price £3.45 (incl. p&p).

**Rev Donald Eadie** is a Methodist minister, formerly a Tutor in Pastoral Theology at Wesley College, Bristol, and Chairman of the Birmingham District of the Methodist Church. He now lives in Birmingham. For nearly nine years he has lived with a serious spinal condition. Donald is now freer to be with people who want to ponder life with its meaning, search for a sense of direction and wonder what God is up to in all this.

**Maureen Edwards**, who served for seven years as a mission partner in Kenya, is the Editor of the annual *Methodist Prayer Handbook*. She has also compiled and edited many books for the International Bible Reading Association. Most of all she values what she has learnt from her many encounters with Christians from many parts of the world.

**Maureen Henderson** trained as a nurse and midwife before working in Zimbabwe. She joined the Community of the Sacred Passion in 1968 and worked in Tanzania. On returning to England in 1979 she became engaged in multi-faith community work in Walsall, West Midlands. Moving to London in 1989 she continued her inter-faith work as part of the South London Industrial Mission. She now lives as a solitary attached to the parish of St Mary and St Nicholas in Leatherhead, Surrey. Maureen is the author of *Friends on the Way: a life enriched by engagement with people of many faiths* (Epworth Press).

**R. A. Henderson,** a Catholic and a Scotswoman, (when talking to herself she addresses herself by her initials) lives in Italy, where she works in the Modern Languages Department of the University of Turin, teaching translation and running a theatre workshop seminar for third and fourth year students. She is also a professional translator, specialising in Gestalt psychotherapy and analysis of Semitic literatures, and often collaborates as a translator/interpreter with the Order of Preachers (the Dominicans), with whom she is closely connected and among whom she has many friends. She is a Eucharistic minister for the sick.

**Commissioner Alex Hughes** is the national leader of The Salvation Army in the United Kingdom with the Republic of Ireland to which he was appointed in 1999. He first became involved in The Salvation Army through Sunday School, and following training he was appointed to various corps (churches) in the UK. He then became a member of staff at the Training College for officers in London before being transferred to the South America West Territory in 1967. Various regional and national appointments followed in several territories, including Mexico and Central America, and South America West. In 1985 the Commissioners were appointed to The Salvation Army's International HQ in London where they served for two and a half years, working in the Americas and Caribbean department. This was followed by national leadership appointments in South America East before returning to London as International Secretary for the Americas and Caribbean. Commissioner Hughes is married with two daughters and one grandson.

**Jan Sutch Pickard** is a Member of the ecumenical Iona Community and a former Vice-President of the Methodist Conference. A writer and local preacher, she has lived, worked and worshipped in Nigeria, Notting Hill and New Mills. For many years she was involved in education relating to the World Church, editing the *Prayer Handbook* and the *Now* and *Connect* magazines. Until recently she has been Deputy Warden of the Iona Community, based at the Macleod Centre, and in September 2001 she will move to the Abbey to become Warden of the Iona Community's work on this small Hebridean island, a place of pilgrimage for thousands of people.

**Rev Julian M. Pursehouse** is a Methodist minister in the Peterborough circuit. He began his ministry in Long Eaton, near Nottingham. After completing his B.A. in Theology at Nottingham University he lectured in Old Testament Studies for the East Midlands Ministry Training Scheme, and was also a Chaplain to the Nottinghamshire Hospice.

**Dr Anthony Reddie** is a Postdoctoral Research Fellow at the Queen's Foundation, in Birmingham. He is also a Consultant in Christian Education and Development to the Methodist Church. Prior to working at Queen's, he undertook doctoral research into the Christian education and nurture of Black children and young people in inner city churches. He is the author of *Growing into Hope,* the first Black African-centred work in Christian Education in Europe. His most recent publication is *Faith Stories and the Experience of Black Elders (Sing the Lord's Song in a Strange Land)* published by Jessica Kingsley, May 2001.

**Rev Canon Pat Robson** is Priest in Charge of the parish of St. Enoder, Cornwall. She is an Honorary Canon of Truro Cathedral and Co-ordinating Director of the White Cross Mission, which is a charity working with abandoned children in Eastern Europe. She has lived in Cornwall for thirty years and has made a specialist study of the lives of the peregrine Celtic saints. Her two books, *The Celtic Heart* and *A Celtic Liturgy* are published by HarperCollins.

**Rev E. Philip Schofield** was a minister of the Congregational Church and also served eighteen years in the RAF. Living in London he and his wife became active in Christian/Jewish relationships and human rights issues, particularly related to the treatment of Jews and Christians in Russia. He was Joint Honorary Secretary of the Council of Christians and Jews. Ventriloquism has been his hobby since boyhood, and, with magic, has been used to great effect in his ministry and to raise money for numerous charities. In his retirement Philip has turned his hand to writing, with some success, and has continued preaching and entertaining. In 2001 he was diagnosed with terminal cancer, to which his response has been: 'My faith is strong. I keep reasonably active and will continue to do so for as long as I can.'

**Professor Peter Stephens** is minister of the Mint Methodist Church in Exeter and Methodist Chaplain to the University of Exeter. He has worked as a circuit minister and college tutor in Manchester, Nottingham, Croydon, Bristol, where he also worked as a city councillor, Birmingham and Plymouth. From 1986 to 1999 he was Professor of Church History at the University of Aberdeen, where he was also Dean of the Faculty of Divinity. He was President of the Methodist Conference 1998-99. He has written on the theology of the continental reformers, Bucer, Bullinger, Luther and Zwingli, and on the Methodist Churches in Europe.

# Acknowledgements

Methodist Publishing House gratefully acknowledges the use of copyright items. Every effort has been made to trace copyright owners, but where we have been unsuccessful we would welcome information which would enable us to make appropriate acknowledgement in any reprint.

Page

7       John White, *Life in the Spirit*, Epworth Press.

8       J. B. Phillips, *Plain Christianity*, Epworth Press.

15      V. L. Edminson, 'He rode at furious speed', *Poems of Today*, Sidgwick & Jackson/Pan Macmillan Ltd. Permission applied for.

17      John Taylor, *The Go-Between God*, SCM Press.

18      Ronald Spivey, *Preacher's Handbook 4*, Epworth Press.

19      Delia Smith, *A Journey Into God*, Spire.

19      Evelyn Underhill, *The Fruits of the Spirit*, Longman, Green & Co.

26      Stella Bristow & Rosemary Wass,' Spirit of God', by permission of the authors.

28      W. E. Sangster, *The Pure in Heart*, Epworth Press.

30   Cecily Taylor, 'The bright wind is blowing', *Textures of Tomorrow*, United Reformed Church, and © Stainer & Bell Limited, London.

30   R. A. Finlayson, *More Sermons I Should Like to Have Preached*, Epworth Press.

37   Peter D. Bishop, *Clinging to Faith*, Epworth Press.

37   James Fenhagen, *Invitation to Holiness*, Harper & Row Publishers Inc.

38   Thomas R. Hawkins, *A Life that Becomes the Gospel*, Upper Room Books.

39   David J. Winwood, *I Want to Begin a Christian Life*, DEY, Methodist Church.

47   Charles V. Bryant, *Discovering Our Spiritual Gifts*, Upper Room Books.

49   Elizabeth Goudge, *The Dean's Watch*, Hodder & Stoughton.

50   Benjamin Drewery, *Oxford Sermons*, Epworth Press.

50   K. G. Egerston, in M. T. Kelsey, *Speaking in Tongues*, Epworth Press.

55   Leslie Weatherhead, *The Significance of Silence*, Epworth Press.

55   Harold S. Darby, *The Grace and the Love*, Epworth Press.

56   Ron DelBene, *The Hunger of the Heart*, Upper Room Books.

57   Joan Puls, *Every Bush is Burning*, WCC Publications, Geneva.

57   Ann Bird, *Called to Care*, Methodist Publishing House.

58   James Kirkup, 'Giving and taking', *The Prodigal Son*, by permission of the author.

66   Michael Durber, 'Praise God for love!' *Textures of Tomorrow*, United Reformed Church, and by permission of the author.

66   Emil Brunner, *Letter to the Romans*, tr. H. A. Kennedy, Lutterworth Press.

67   Christine Walters, 'God of the pilgrim way', by permission of the author.

83   Kate Compston, *Leaves from the Tree of Peace*, United Reformed Church, and by permission of the author.

85   Julie M. Hulme, *The Light beyond the Wall: Poems from praying in dark places*, the Bethany Project, 1991, and by permission of the author.

87   William Barclay, 'O God, my Father', *The Doubleday Prayer Collection*, Mary Bachelor, Lion Publishing. Permission applied for.

95   Bernard Thorogood, 'Spirit of endless compassion', *A Restless Hope, The URC Prayer Handbook* 1995, United Reformed Church, and by permission of the author.

96   Judith Pinhey, *The Music of Love*, HarperCollins. Permission applied for.

150 Fred Kaan, 'Help us to accept each other,' © Stainer & Bell Limited, London.

152 Donald Hilton, 'Reach out my hand', *Textures of Tomorrow*, United Reformed Church, and by permission of the author.

154 Roy Niblett, 'Two Kinds of Knowledge', *Epworth Review*, May 1990.

160 Ida Church, *The Homely Year*, Epworth Press.

169 Alan Gaunt, 'In all our attitudes', *Leaves from the Tree of Peace*, United Reformed Church, and © Stainer & Bell Limited, London.

170 Leslie Church, *The Homely Year*, Epworth Press.

173 Denis Vernon, by permission of the author.

180 Anthony Bridge, BBC World Service *Reflections* script 1986, in *Celebrating Friendship*, Brian Frost and Pauline Webb, Epworth Press.

182-3 David Jenkins, 'Holy Spirit', *The Power and the Glory: The URC Prayer Handbook* 1987, United Reformed Church, and by permission of the author.